Adventures in
Slow Cooking

Adventures in Slow Cooking

120 SLOW-COOKER RECIPES FOR PEOPLE WHO LOVE FOOD

Sarah DiGregorio

PHOTOGRAPHY BY ANDREW PURCELL

WM

WILLIAM MORROW

An Imprint of HarperCollinsPublishers

ADVENTURES IN SLOW COOKING. Copyright © 2017 by
Sarah DiGregorio. Foreword © 2017 by Grant Achatz.

HarperCollins books may be purchased for educational, business, or sales
promotional use. For information, please email the Special Markets Department
at SPsales@harpercollins.com.

FIRST EDITION

Designed by Renata De Oliveira

Photography © Andrew Purcell

Food styling by Carrie Purcell

Prop styling by Paige Hicks

Illustration on page xv courtesy of the US Patent and Trademark Office

Library of Congress Cataloging-in-Publication Data has been applied
for.

ISBN 978-0-06-266137-1

17 18 19 20 21   QDG   10 9 8 7 6 5 4 3 2 1

For Amol and Mira,
who were willing to
share one small Brooklyn
apartment with six slow
cookers. You're the best.
I love you.

Contents

Foreword

Slow cookers have baggage. They're associated with 1970s cooking, beef stew and pot roast, chili and casseroles. So maybe it's a surprise to find my name here, a modernist chef writing a foreword to a slow-cooker book.

It shouldn't be. In the top-tier restaurant world, we are all about slow cooking. Sometimes the technique goes by another name—like *sous vide*—but the idea is the same. Gentle, low, long cooking. The slow cooker can bring the depth of flavor, rich textures, and aromas found at the best restaurants into your home kitchen.

I'll give you an example. At my restaurant Next, we re-created the French Laundry menu from one night in 1996 when I ate there with my father. And one of the iconic canapés that we included was Thomas Keller's truffle-infused custard served in an eggshell with a potato chip on top. We actually used a slow cooker to steam the custards. Because there's no better way. We have so much technology in my kitchens, but at the end of the day, sometimes the best way to do something is with a fifty-dollar slow cooker from Amazon.

It's not a thermal circulator. It doesn't cost a fortune. But it is a very useful tool in the modern kitchen. Just because it was popular with your parents in the 1970s and '80s doesn't mean it doesn't have a place in modern cooking. Historically, when you look at gastronomy, some of the best dishes in the world are items that are covered and cooked slowly, bubbling away.

Tools are tools, and once you know what a slow cooker does well—steaming, acting as a water bath, braising—you can use it in a regimented way to great effect. It reminds me of when I started at the French Laundry in 1996, soon after that memorable dinner with my father. I got to my station and there was a microwave there. I recoiled; I thought this is terrible—but of course it wasn't. You have to remove your value judgments and think about it as a tool, nothing more. The only relevant question is, what can it do?

To bring the slow cooker into the modern kitchen, you should be conscious of the order in which you add ingredients. The old idea of throwing everything in the pot at once and walking away generally isn't going to result in great food. Long, slow cooking will mellow flavors, so in many cases, adding more herbs, spices, or acid toward the end of the cook time will wake up the food, and the aroma of those ingredients will be intense, activated by steam. Throw in a bouquet of thyme or rosemary in the last twenty minutes of cooking, or finish a dish with spices infused in butter. Those aromatics will perfume the whole dish in a potent way, blending the long-cooked with the immediate, and that's an amazing thing.

What's fair game? Everything that benefits from being cooked to tenderness. That includes vegetables, which are often overlooked by slow-cooker cookbooks. But think about fennel cooked in olive oil until it's melting and sweet, cherry tomatoes caramelized in their own juices, or eggplant braised in harissa and honey. Whole grains can be steamed in the slow cooker or simmered with other ingredients for a risotto or ragout. And there's no better way to make silky custards—both savory and sweet—than in a slow-cooker water bath.

So let go of your preconceived ideas about slow-cooker cooking and let this book be a guide as you seek to answer that central question, the only one that matters: What can this tool do?

—*Grant Achatz*

Introduction: Thoughts about Slow Cooking

In some corners of the food media world, where I worked until I started this book, there's a low-level snobbery about slow cookers. I was guilty of it, too. So many slow-cooker recipes seemed to promise more than they could deliver or were stuck in Condensed Soup Land. For me, that changed when I worked on a story about slow-cooker recipes for *Food & Wine* with Grant Achatz. (He was kind enough to write the foreword to this book.) Listening to him excitedly rattle off all the dishes a slow cooker could make (*barbacoa* and steamed British pudding; whole grains and dumplings!) made me really excited to go home, dust off my slow cooker, and take it for a spin. I made perfect polenta without stirring once, and then a velvety *pot de crème*, and I was hooked.

The idea for this book came out of those conversations with Grant—and specifically, the sense of excitement that came with them. Whether you're a slow-cooker skeptic or someone who uses a slow cooker all the time, what I would most like to convey is that sense of fun—the joy of tinkering with this underestimated gadget.

This is a slow-cooker book for people who love to cook. It's not all about getting out of the kitchen as quickly as possible at any cost to the finished dish. I love being in the kitchen,

and I want to use my (sometimes limited) time there efficiently and well. Some of the recipes in this book are fast and easy, some are one-pot meals, and all of them are realistic. But with a few exceptions, I'm not a fan of setting and forgetting—by which I mean putting raw ingredients in the slow cooker and then eating them ten hours later without doing anything else. In most cases, dishes cooked that way will be underwhelming; they'll lack vivid flavor and texture.

So you'll notice that most of these recipes have steps to take before you slow-cook and then just before you eat that build layers of flavor: Sauté aromatics before you go to work, for example, or broil before serving to add caramelization. Simple techniques like those can make slow-cook dishes taste as vibrant and alive as the food you cook on your stovetop. Often, these upgrades take a matter of minutes. (And if you need a set-it-and-forget-it recipe, I suggest duck confit, which is just about the easiest, most forgiving dish in this book.)

Some of these recipes can cook (or can hold on warm) all day or all night, and I've marked those for you so you can find them when you need them. But some of them cook for only a few hours, because I'd like to broaden the way you think about your slow cooker. The ability

to cook unattended for eight to ten hours is just *one* of the slow cooker's advantages. Pour a little water into the bottom and it's a bain-marie, or water bath, perfect for gently cooking custards. (I'll never make a custard any other way ever again.) It saves a burner during the holidays; it cooks without heating the kitchen in the summer. It uses far less energy than the oven, and it can steam a perfect batch of whole grains while you're on a conference call. It creates a cooking environment that's dense with moisture, trapping flavorful steam almost like a tagine. Wrap a big hunk of chile-rubbed lamb in banana leaves, and the slow cooker will braise it as slowly and gently as an earthen barbecue pit. And, yes, it can make pho and cassoulet and polenta and congee while you're at work.

I've tried to walk a line between excellence and expediency throughout, which is a line I think we all walk all the time. Sometimes you plan a dinner party for fun and sometimes you just need a supersimple dish of beans and kale on a night when you've worked late. The mix of recipes is designed for real life.

And I'd like to push back a little against slow-cooker snobbery in general. Let's be honest: The slow cooker became popular because it made it possible for women to do something other than check the roast all afternoon. And maybe that association with female home cooks has something to do with the slow cooker's place in the culinary pecking order.

My first encounter with a slow cooker was through my grandmother. My grandparents lived in a creaky old house in Topeka, Kansas, where they moved when they retired and sold their family farm out on the prairie. The house had a big garden in the backyard where my grandparents grew tomatoes and carrots and roses. It had an old wooden ice-cream maker with an iron handle that all the cousins took turns cranking. And in the kitchen, of course, there was a slow cooker, which my grandmother used to make pot roast with carrots. She cooked the pot roast all day, while she cleaned, worked, gardened, or went to church, and the small house filled with the most delicious, promising aroma. By the time we sat down to eat, the pot roast was a little dry and the carrots were mushy. But it was delicious in the way that slightly overcooked pot roast can be, especially when it's made by your grandmother. And here's the thing: My grandmother was a great cook. But she was also a farm woman and a nurse, and on her feet all day, and if the pot roast was a little dry, well, so be it. She had things to worry about, and the utter perfection of dinner wasn't one of them. (Here I feel the need to reassure you that modern slow cookers have an automatic warm setting that helps prevent overcooking.)

I know this is not an unusual story. That's why slow cookers have a nostalgic pull. They are our parents' food, our grandparents' food. They are love and a busy life, work and family dinners. So as much as I am seeking to update, improve, and modernize slow-cooker cooking, I have huge respect for what the slow cooker means—and for the women who were able to do something else while the roast cooked.

The Birth of the Slow Cooker

The story of the slow cooker begins in a small Lithuanian village in the mid-1800s. There, every Friday afternoon, a little girl named Tamara Kaslovski Nachumsohn was dispatched by her mother with a big pot of uncooked cholent, a rich bean stew, to the bakery's communal oven. Tamara's soup pot went into the oven on Friday, along with all the soup pots of her neighbors. At sundown, the baker banked the oven's fire and went home to observe the Jewish Sabbath. All Friday night and all day Saturday, the cholent simmered away in the gentle, fading heat of the unattended oven. Around sundown on Saturday, Tamara and her neighbors went back to the bakery to fetch their pots of stew for dinner.

Fast forward to 1936 Chicago: A professional inventor named Irving Nachumsohn (he later changed his name to Naxon) remembered his mother, Tamara, telling him about this ingenious way of cooking cholent completely unattended. So he invented a "cooking apparatus" designed to mimic the conditions in that long-ago, faraway bakery oven: an electric heating element wrapped around an insulated, lidded pot, all of it housed in an outer casing.

He may have invented it with bean stew in mind, but Nachumsohn imagined his apparatus as having almost limitless possibilities in the kitchen. In the patent application, which was granted in 1940, he wrote: "One object in my invention is to provide an improved cooking means capable of meeting the diversified phases in the general art of cooking, such as baking, searing, scalloping, steaming, stewing and so forth."

Nachumsohn, who also invented the telesign (the scrolling signs you see in Times Square), the electric frying pan, and a washing machine for doll clothes, marketed his invention as the Naxon Beanery and sold it throughout the 1950s and '60s. In 1970, he sold the invention to the Rival Company, which rebranded the gadget as the Crock-Pot.

Although there have been cosmetic changes to slow cookers in the intervening years, the core technology really hasn't changed. It's still an electric cooking element wrapped around an insulated pot, housed in a casing. Your slow cooker is really a Naxon Beanery.

How Your Slow Cooker Works

A slow cooker is made up of two basic parts: The first is the outer casing, or base, which contains the control panel and the hidden electric heating coils that wrap around the bottom and sides. Then there's the insert, or crock, in which you put your food; it's usually a heavy stoneware pot similar to a Dutch oven. Then, of course, there's the lid. That's pretty much it—slow cookers haven't changed a lot since they were invented.

I wish I could say that every slow cooker has a standardized temperature for warm, low, and high settings, but they vary among brands and models. For reference, this is a very generalized guide.

WARM: 155°F to 165°F
LOW: 175°F to 190°F
HIGH: 200°F to 212°F

However, your mileage may vary! I conducted an experiment in which I put eight cups of 70°F water (cool water out of my tap) into three new six-quart slow cookers from three different common brands; let's call them

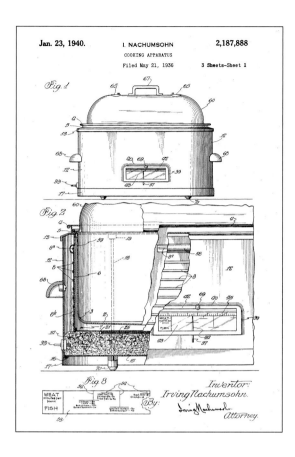

Fig. 1

Fig. 2

Fig. 8

MEAT
minutes per
pound

FISH

Inventor:
Irving Nachumsohn.
By
Attorney.

cookers A, B, and C. I turned on the cookers to low heat, and after one hour cooker A was at 152°F, cooker B was at 125°F, and cooker C was at 120°F. After about three hours, the difference between cookers A and C had evened out, and they were both chugging away at about 180°F, where they stayed. That is a great temperature for long braising—well below the boiling point, which is 212°F. Cooker B, however, continued to climb, and while cookers A and C held the lower temperature, cooker B set on low ended up all the way up at 210°F after eight hours. I then decreased the heat on all of them to warm, which is the setting that should hold your food at a safe temperature until you're ready to eat without overcooking it. Both cookers A and C dipped down to 158°F, which is a food-safe but not-too-high temperature. Cooker B actually jumped from 210°F to 212°F when I set it on warm (now it was at a full, rolling boil) before falling down to 180°F, which is too hot for holding food.

On the other hand, some older, vintage slow cookers run quite a bit cooler than the new ones I was working with. That's because there's a recent emphasis on (or paranoia about) food safety. Some of the older models didn't heat up quickly enough, leaving foods too long in the temperature range where bacteria can grow. The general, simplified rule of thumb is that you don't want any food to be between 40°F and 140°F for longer than four hours. Below 40°F and above 140°F are the safe ranges for holding food for longer periods of time.

So the moral is this: Get a probe thermometer (they are inexpensive and extremely useful) and get to know your slow cooker's temperament by filling it halfway with cold water and then monitoring the temperature over the course of several hours. Remember two things: First, for food safety, you want the water temperature to rise well above 140°F well before four hours elapse. Second, water boils at 212°F, and that's too hot for long, slow braising—if your slow cooker hits 212°F while on low heat, it runs hot. If you know it runs quite hot, you will want to err on the side of shorter cooking times. (Or, frankly, if you slow-cook a lot, it might be worth getting a new one that doesn't run hot, like one of the models I recommend below.) If it is a vintage model and runs cool, you may want to start foods on high to get the temperature up more quickly before reducing to low, if that's the setting the recipe calls for.

Buying a Slow Cooker

I did not test every single slow cooker that is on the market (there are hundreds), but I did a lot of research on the most popular brands and models and regularly tested with six different models (and had recipe testers try the recipes with still others). Here are three essential takeaways.

THE MOST VERSATILE SIZE IS SIX-QUART OVAL.

Yes, that's on the large side, but it's easier to use a larger cooker for smaller quantities than the other way around. I find that cooking moderate amounts of food (say, four servings) in a six-quart cooker works very well, and the additional space means that you can sometimes get nice browning, which is not something you can always count on in a slow cooker. (The Chipotle-Almond Braised Beef Tacos on page 135 are a great example of this; the beef gets a nice crust on it.)

FOR BEST RESULTS, YOU NEED A PROGRAMMABLE COOKER WITH AN AUTOMATIC SWITCH TO WARM.

That rules out the models with the knob with which you have to manually switch the heat. The newer programmable models allow you to set them to cook for a certain amount of time on either low or high heat. After that time has elapsed, the cooker automatically switches to warm, which should then gradually drop the temperature to 160°F at most and hold it there. Food will still overcook if you leave it on warm for too long, but that setting is invaluable for a gap of an hour or so between when the food is done and when you get home. (And each recipe indicates how long it is advisable, from a taste point of view, to leave it on warm.) Without that automatic switch to warm, your cooker will just keep bubbling away on low or high until you turn it off.

IT'S NICE, BUT NOT AT ALL NECESSARY, TO HAVE A SLOW COOKER THAT ALLOWS YOU TO SEAR DIRECTLY IN THE INSERT.

Some cookers have an insert that has a searing or a browning function: This allows you to brown meat or sauté aromatics directly in the insert, either with the insert set on a stovetop burner or in the cooker on a browning setting. This is really great for saving a pan to wash, but these cookers tend to be more expensive. And, anecdotally, I've heard that the nonstick coatings on them can bubble or flake with heavy use—you have to be careful not to use metal cooking implements or steel wool on them. Still, the convenience factor of using only one pan to sear and then slow-cook is pretty fantastic, and if you use your slow cooker quite often for main dishes, this feature might be worth it to you. **You'll notice all the recipes in this book are written for slow cookers that do *not* have a searing or browning function. If you happen to have one, simply disregard the direction to cook in a skillet and use your insert instead. That might require you to reorder a step or two, so please read through the method first, and if there's a step that directs to sauté or brown before slow cooking, just do that in your slow cooker before you add anything else.**

If you're in the market for a new slow cooker, I'd recommend one of the following three choices.

The best overall is the **KitchenAid 6-Quart Slow Cooker with Glass Lid** (list price is about $100). I love it because it runs very, very low and slow—to me, the biggest problem with modern slow cookers is that they run too hot. KitchenAid's low setting is truly low: It reaches only about 180°F and then steadily holds there, thanks to an internal thermostat that makes small adjustments to keep the temperature constant. (Most slow cookers don't have this.) When the warm setting kicks in, it eventually falls all the way to 147°F. (If you are cooking with this model, whenever there is a temperature range in a recipe, know that you should plan for the longer cook time.) It also has special insulation that prevents hot spots and doesn't scorch the outsides of delicate dishes like stratas, which feels like a minor miracle. Additionally, the control panel is a joy—extremely intuitive to set and easy to read. The handles on the insert stay relatively cool while cooking. There's an alarm when the cook time has elapsed. This is a basic model—and you do need to remember that it runs slower than most—but it does everything right.

My second-favorite is the **Hamilton Beach 6-Quart Programmable Stovetop Slow Cooker** (list price about $80). This model has a nonstick-coated aluminum insert, which is much lighter and easier to wash than the traditional stone crocks—but more to the point, it's also stovetop safe. It works just as well as a skillet for sautéing aromatics or browning meat. So you can sauté on the stovetop and then transfer to the casing to slow-cook. I only wish it had more bottom surface area—to avoid crowding the pan, you'll likely need to sear meat in batches. It also offers nice, even low heat without hot spots and a wonderfully intuitive control panel.

Then I have a slightly irrational favorite: It's the **All-Clad Gourmet 7-Quart Slow Cooker with All-in-One Browning** (list price about $300, though you can usually find it discounted). Like the Hamilton Beach, this comes with a nonstick-coated aluminum insert, but you can use this one either on the stovetop or with the slow cooker's browning setting. There are a few notable downsides to this cooker, including the price and the fact that it won't let you program fewer than four hours for the low setting and two hours for the high setting. (I believe this is a kind of paternal attempt to make sure you are following food safety rules.) It also runs a bit hot, around 200°F on low. But it has a very major upside, and that is that its searing and browning ability is the best of any I tried. The insert is wider and shallower than most others, with lots of surface area—five chicken thighs fit easily without crowding. Turned to 400°F, it gets screamingly hot, enough that chicken skin sizzles violently on contact. Set to 350°F, it perfectly sautés an onion. If you (like most people) most often use your slow cooker for main dishes that require sautéing aromatics first or browning meat, it's worth considering an investment in this slow cooker—especially if you really hate doing dishes. It also has an internal thermostat like the KitchenAid does, so it holds a steady temperature. It's also really good-looking. But if you use your cooker for items like frittatas and cakes that cook for less time than four hours, then it might not be worth the money, both because of the timing quirk and because of the shape of the insert.

What about the Instant Pot?

The Instant Pot is a multi-cooker—it has settings for pressure cooking, slow cooking, sautéing, and yogurt making, and it can probably do your taxes, too. It's a very cool appliance, but I don't think it's as good at slow cooking as traditional slow cookers are. That's because the lid seals and locks in place—as it must for pressure cooking—which allows for even less evaporation than traditional slow cookers. In some circumstances, that means a dish ends up swimming in liquid when you translate a traditional slow-cooker recipe to slow cooking in the Instant Pot. (The locking lid also means you can't use a probe thermometer and close the lid over it—not the end of the world, but not ideal.) I also find the control panel not at all intuitive, though of course you can figure it out once you fiddle with it for a while.

To further confuse matters, the Instant Pot also has three slow-cooker heat settings (not counting warm): **less** (180°F to 190°F), **normal** (190°F to 200°F), and **more** (200°F to 210°F). Those do not exactly correspond to the heat settings on most other slow cookers—although the "less" setting seems like it would be the same as low, it seems to run much slower. Instant Pot *does* have an auto-switch to warm, as does a traditional slow cooker.

All that said, if you have an Instant Pot, yes, you can use the slow cooker setting to make many of the recipes in this book, with a few caveats.

- The manufacturer claims the Instant Pot's "less" setting runs at about 180°F, but I don't think I believe them. (And I can't use a probe thermometer to find out for sure because of the way the lid locks into place.) The "less" setting runs very, very slow. If you're looking to stretch out a cooking time, try the "less" setting where "low" is called for, and increase the cooking time by an hour or so. But the better analog is the "normal" setting: In general, use the "normal" setting for when "low" is called for and the "more" setting where "high" is called for.

- If the finished product is quite dependent on a certain ratio of liquid in the dish (as in polenta), try reducing the cooking liquid slightly, by about 15 to 20 percent, to compensate for the complete lack of evaporation.

Getting the Most Out of Your Slow Cooker: Flavors and Ingredients

Long cooking softens flavors. Think, for example, about the difference between freshly grated garlic and garlic confit. Or think of the way a long roast transforms fennel from crunchy, vegetal, and sharp to silky and sweet. Cooking ingredients for a long time tends to marry and mellow flavors, but you also want the finished dish to have oomph: balanced and varied flavors and textures. I think when we say something is delicious, we mean that there's a certain tension in the dish—a push-pull of sweet and salty, tart or herbaceous and rich, crunchy and soft. The tension between or the balance among the flavors is what makes the dish vivid, and a slow cooker can bring homogeneity to otherwise distinct ingredients.

So here are a few rules for thinking about flavor when using your slow cooker.

1. USE BIG FLAVOR (MORE THAN YOU WOULD OTHERWISE).

It's helpful (and logical) to start with ingredients that can stand up to long cooking—flavors that can take a little mellowing and actually be improved by it. That can be as simple as a big dose of ginger and garlic or a spoonful of fennel seeds and red pepper flakes or a handful of pickled peppers. But keep in mind that as a general rule you can use a larger quantity of big-flavor ingredients than you normally would, because their intensity will mellow.

2. ADD INGREDIENTS AT DIFFERENT STAGES.

There's no rule that says that everything has to go into the cooker at the same time. In fact, it's better to add ingredients at different intervals. For instance, for Spicy Kimchi and Pork Ramen (page 128), I add most of the kimchi at the very beginning, but then add a little bit more just before the soup is done to add back some of the tart intensity that's been cooked out of the first batch. Similarly, in Farro Puttanesca (page 90) the tomato-y farro is cooked with garlic, fennel, and red pepper flakes for three hours, and then right before serving, I bloom more fennel seeds and red pepper flakes in olive oil and stir that in for a more immediate, fragrant pop of flavor. You can do this with fresh herbs, too—stirring in a handful of chopped herbs in the last few minutes will wake a dish right up.

3. BEFORE SERVING, TASTE FOR SALT, SOUR, SWEET, FRESHNESS, AND RICHNESS.

Everyone knows to taste for salt before serving, and you certainly should do that, but taste for all the other variables that make a dish delicious, too. A last-minute squeeze of lemon or drop of vinegar can do wonders, but so can a drizzle of olive oil or honey if a dish is feeling too austere or sharp. I suggest a version of this in most of these recipes—braise eggplant in harissa and honey, for example, and then before serving, stir in more harissa and honey. It's a simple finishing step that takes literally seconds, but it makes a huge difference. So I can't emphasize it enough: If you taste a dish straight out of the slow cooker and it isn't delicious, it's probably mellowed out too much. First add a bit of salt, and then think about the seasonings that are already in it (herbs, citrus, vinegar, sweetener, spices) and add more of those elements, just a little at a time, until it tastes good to you.

Getting the Most Out of Your Slow Cooker: Techniques

Moisture is key to the slow cooker's strengths. The way it traps moisture makes it great at braising, steaming, poaching, and acting as a water bath. But it can also be a problem. That's because every fresh ingredient has moisture, and in the closed slow cooker, little of it evaporates. If you put fresh vegetables and/or meat in the slow cooker with some broth, for example, when it's done you're going to have more liquid than you started with. That's why I sometimes add very little or no liquid at the start—in the slow cooker, everything is self-saucing.

Here are four techniques you'll find throughout this book that are designed to control moisture and make sure you don't end up with a watery dish.

1. SAUTÉ AROMATICS.

I really wish you could just throw raw diced onion in the slow cooker, but you generally can't. If you do, the onions will retain a weirdly crunchy texture while also giving off a *ton* of liquid that will swamp the dish. That's why I nearly always sauté onion, garlic, and other aromatics before adding them to the cooker.

2. SOAK UP CONDENSATION BY LINING THE LID.

When you're using the slow cooker as a water bath for delicate custards and the like, place a double layer of paper towels over the top of the cooker before closing the lid on top (see photo). The paper towels soak up the steam and prevent it from dripping back down onto the surface of the custards. You could also use a kitchen towel, but I like that paper towels are both absorbent and thin enough to allow the lid to close tightly.

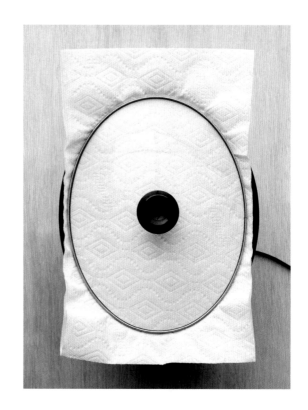

3. SET THE LID AJAR TO LET MOISTURE ESCAPE ENTIRELY.

In certain cases and/or for short periods of time, you can use the slow cooker with the lid set ajar or removed entirely. The manufacturers don't want you to do this because without the lid, they can't ensure raw food gets hot enough to be safe to eat. So I use this technique sparingly, as with toasting granola or Chex mix or reducing liquid at the end of cooking. You should not, for example, put raw meat in the cooker and then set the lid ajar while cooking it.

Slow cooking mellows flavors;
use citrus and herbs to wake up
a dish before serving.

Before serving, taste for more than just salt—think about the seasonings that are already in the dish and add a little bit more of those tart, rich, spicy, or sweet ingredients until the dish tastes vivid.

CLOCKWISE, FROM TOP: feta, harissa, Parmesan, olives, chile flakes, olive oil, fennel, honey

4. DON'T PUT FROZEN FOODS INTO THE SLOW COOKER.

Always defrost and drain frozen foods before putting them in the slow cooker. This is for two reasons: First, frozen foods contain water, and defrosting and draining first prevents that water from diluting the dish. Second, and most important, frozen foods will prevent the temperature of the food from rising quickly enough as it cooks, and that's a food safety issue.

Getting the Most Out of Your Slow Cooker: Tools

These tools and tricks make it possible to slow-cook and serve efficiently and well.

1. TO CHECK THE TEMPERATURE WITHOUT OPENING THE LID, USE A PROBE THERMOMETER.

Avoid opening the slow cooker while it's cooking because you'll lose heat, causing the dish to take longer to cook than expected. Peeking once or twice, especially to stir, is not the end of the world, but you want to avoid opening the lid when it's not directed in the recipe. The best solution is using a probe thermometer. That way you can, for example, stick the probe end into a whole chicken or a meatball, close the slow-cooker lid over the cord, and set the thermometer to alarm when the food hits the desired internal temperature. It's the best and easiest way to use a slow cooker with precision—you can find out exactly how hot or cool your cooker is running without ever opening the lid.

2. USE BAKEWARE AND OTHER VESSELS.

You can use your slow cooker as a water bath for making custards or as a steam oven for cakes—you just need bakeware that fits in the insert. Anything that's oven-safe is fair game. Ramekins, either four or eight ounces, are extremely useful for custards and puddings, as are eight-ounce canning jars, and a baking dish or loaf pan is great for steamed cakes and cheesecakes. And the presentation is pretty, too.

3. USE A FOIL COLLAR TO PREVENT DELICATE DISHES FROM BURNING.

On most cookers, the hottest spot is a thin strip all around the bottom of the side of the insert and, in particular, the side that is opposite (farthest from) the control panel. It might also be the two narrow curved sides on an oval slow cooker. Luckily, there's an easy fix. When you're cooking anything that might be at risk of burning against the side (like a frittata or a cake that's baked directly in the insert), just put a folded strip of foil around the sides of the insert (see photos on the next page). You can do it on only one side or both, depending on your slow cooker's temperament. The foil will act as insulation and prevent overbrowning.

Useful equipment: a probe thermometer for slow cooking with precision and bakeware that fits inside the slow cooker

How to Insulate with a Foil Collar

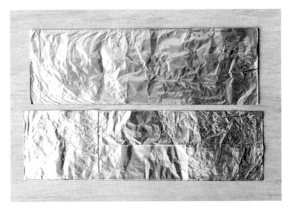

1. To make a foil collar, fold a piece of foil so it's about 12 inches long and 3 inches wide. Repeat if you plan to line both sides of your cooker.

2. Use the piece of foil to line the side of the insert that runs the hottest; it's most likely the wall of the insert opposite (farthest from) the control panel. For most recipes, like a strata or spaghetti pie, you will only need to line one side. You'll then line with parchment (see next page), and the food you add to the cooker will hold the foil in place.

3. If your slow cooker runs particularly hot or if you are cooking a cake directly in the insert (such as the Cardamom-Molasses Apple Upside-Down Cake on page 212), you will want to line both sides to prevent burning. Simply repeat the process on the other side.

4. LINE WITH PARCHMENT FOR EASIER CLEANUP AND MORE ATTRACTIVE SERVING.

Lots of people like to use plastic slow-cooker liners, but they are expensive, especially since they can only be used once. And they're not nonstick. (And something about cooking directly in plastic is a little unappetizing to me.) Instead, simply line your slow cooker with parchment paper and then trim the top so the lid can close. This makes it so much easier to remove dishes that are baked directly in the insert, like frittatas and cakes—just reach in, grab the edges of the parchment liner, and carefully lift the whole thing out. And it also makes cleanup much faster. You can use foil in exactly the same way, but it will need to be well greased, whereas parchment is a one-step process.

How to Line a Slow Cooker with Parchment

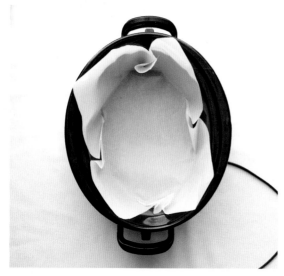

1. Fit a sheet of parchment into the slow cooker. You will need to crumple, press, and fold it to fit, and that's fine.

2. Using scissors, trim the parchment wherever it will prevent the lid from closing. Make sure it comes up at least 2 inches on all sides, so that food doesn't run between the parchment and the slow cooker.

Finding Ingredients

I know I call for ingredients that your closest supermarket may not carry. It's always better to shop from small business owners, so if you have markets in your area that carry Latin American or Asian products, check them first and keep your money in your community. But I admit that even though I live in New York, it can be a hike to find certain ingredients, so I use Amazon for lots of nonperishables, like *za'atar* and Sichuan peppercorns. I find the prices reasonable and the delivery very prompt. I also like Temple of Thai (templeofthai.com) for banana leaves (and really terrific stone mortar and pestles). The Mala Market (themalamarket.com) is great for Sichuan ingredients. If you can find an Indian grocery store, buy a year's supply of spices—you'll find them generally fresher than those sold at other stores (high turnover) and extremely affordable. These shops usually carry a wide variety of spices, not just the ones you might think of as exclusively Indian. So even if you only use garam masala once a year, it's worth stopping in at a Patel Brothers (or another Indian grocery) to get the spices you use most often, because I guarantee you can get a big bag of black peppercorns or fennel seeds at a fraction of the price you'd pay elsewhere. Penzeys (penzeys.com) is also a good source for excellent-quality spices like smoked paprika and vanilla beans.

IF YOU HAVE QUESTIONS ABOUT OR ISSUES WITH ANY OF THESE RECIPES, PLEASE EMAIL ME: ADVENTURESINSLOWCOOKING1@GMAIL.COM.

Barley

Spelt

Farro

Steamed whole grains make a foundation for quick and easy dinner bowls. (Completed bowl recipes start on page 80.)

Basics and Building Blocks

Maybe this says a little too much about me, but I feel most secure in life when I have stock in the freezer. When you have good stock on hand, you're only twenty minutes away from a good meal, even if it's just tortellini in broth with a squeeze of lemon juice. Likewise, a zip-top bag of steamed farro or spelt in the fridge is money in the weeknight dinner bank: Stir-fry it with kimchi or just top it with whatever you have in the fridge. (See page 80 for some of my favorite no-cook grain-bowl ideas.)

My point is that convenience comes in many forms. Most people think a slow cooker is a time-saving tool because you can leave it on to make dinner while you're at work—and that's true—but it can be convenient in other ways, too. It makes wonderful stock. It can make a freezer batch of tomato sauce while you sleep. It can steam whole grains for a week's worth of lunches on a Sunday afternoon. So let's start here, with basics and building blocks that simplify your life and keep good food within easy reach.

*All-day recipes: These recipes can cook or hold on warm unattended for 8 hours or more.

Stocks and Broths

Parmesan-Garlic Broth, 4

24-Hour Beef Stock, 3

Classic Chicken Stock, 5

24-Hour Beef Stock

This is a classic, clean-tasting beef stock. Combine a few cups of this stock with a few cups of the Big-Batch Caramelized Onions (page 10) and simmer for a few minutes for a quick (and also very slow) French onion soup.

5 pounds beef marrow bones

3 celery stalks, quartered

2 large red or yellow onions, quartered

1 large carrot, quartered

1 garlic head, cut in half crosswise through the equator

1 tablespoon tomato paste

½ cup dry red wine

10 fresh flat-leaf parsley sprigs

4 fresh thyme sprigs

2 bay leaves

5 whole cloves

1 teaspoon black peppercorns

1. Preheat the oven to 450°F. Spread the marrow bones out on a rimmed baking sheet and roast until sizzling and starting to brown, 20 minutes.

2. Add the celery, onions, carrot, and garlic to the pan, flip the bones, and toss the vegetables with the fat that's rendered into the pan. Roast until the bones are very deeply browned, about 30 more minutes. Using tongs, transfer the bones and vegetables to a 6- to 8-quart slow cooker. Discard all but a thin slick of the fat from the pan.

3. Put the baking sheet on the stovetop over medium heat. (Set it down over a burner.) Add the tomato paste and cook, stirring constantly with a spatula, until the tomato paste is fragrant, about 30 seconds. Add the wine and cook, scraping up all the browned bits on the pan, until the wine is bubbling, about 1 minute. Tip the contents of the pan into the slow cooker.

4. Add the remaining ingredients to the slow cooker and pour in 10 cups cool water. Cover and cook on HIGH for 2 hours, then reduce to LOW for 22 hours.

5. Using a ladle, skim and discard any foam on the top of the stock. Line a fine-mesh strainer with cheesecloth and pour the stock through the strainer into a large container or bowl. I find it easiest to put a large plastic container into the sink, set the strainer on top, and ladle the stock from the insert into the strainer. Once the liquid level in the slow cooker has gone down, use tongs to remove the bones and vegetables and discard them. At this point, it's easier to pick up the insert and pour the remaining liquid into the strainer. Cool the stock, then store in an airtight container in the refrigerator for up to 4 days or in the freezer for up to 6 months.

ALL-DAY	Holds well on warm through step 4	Prep time: 1 hour (mostly inactive)	Slow-cook time: 24 hours
		Finish time: 10 minutes	Equipment: 6- to 8-quart slow cooker and cheesecloth

Parmesan-Garlic Broth

You can save and freeze your Parmesan rinds for a few months to get the quantity called for here, or you can ask any store that makes grated Parmesan if they'll sell you their rinds. Many Whole Foods or Italian markets will do this. They might even give them to you for free.

10 to 12 ounces Parmesan cheese rinds

5 large garlic cloves, smashed

3 fresh flat-leaf parsley sprigs

2 bay leaves

2 fresh thyme sprigs

1 large yellow or red onion, quartered

2 teaspoons black peppercorns

1 teaspoon white wine vinegar

1. Combine all the ingredients in a 5- to 8-quart slow cooker and add 8 cups cool water. Cover and cook on **HIGH** until the broth is very flavorful, 6 to 8 hours.

2. Strain the broth through a fine-mesh strainer into a large container or bowl. I find it easiest to put a large plastic container into the sink, set the strainer on top, and ladle the broth from the insert into the strainer. Cool the broth, then store in an airtight container in the refrigerator for up to 4 days or in the freezer for up to 6 months.

ALL-DAY	Holds well on warm through step 1	Prep time: 5 minutes	Slow-cook time: 6 to 8 hours
		Finish time: 5 minutes	Equipment: 5- to 8-quart slow cooker

See the photo on page 2.

Classic Chicken Stock

MAKES ABOUT 8 CUPS

I use wings here because they're rich in collagen, which gives the stock full body and flavor. (Because of that collagen, this stock will gel when you chill it.) But you can also use an equivalent weight of chicken (or turkey) carcasses that you've saved and frozen after making roast chicken, or you can use fresh chicken backs. This is an all-purpose stock, the most useful and versatile of the 3 stocks in this chapter.

3 pounds chicken wings

3 celery stalks, quartered

3 garlic cloves, smashed

2 medium carrots, quartered

2 thyme sprigs

1 large yellow or red onion, quartered

1 teaspoon black peppercorns

Generous handful of fresh flat-leaf parsley sprigs

1. Combine all the ingredients in a 6- to 8-quart slow cooker and add 8 cups cool water. Cover and cook on LOW for 10 hours.

2. Using a ladle, skim and discard any foam from the top of the stock. Line a fine-mesh strainer with cheesecloth and pour the stock through the strainer into a large container or bowl. I find it easiest to put a large plastic container into the sink, set the strainer on top, and ladle the stock from the insert into the strainer. Once the liquid level has gone down, use tongs to remove the wings and vegetables and discard them. At this point, it's easier to pick up the insert and pour the remaining liquid into the strainer. Cool the stock, then store in an airtight container in the refrigerator for up to 4 days or in the freezer for up to 6 months.

ALL-DAY	Holds well on warm through step 1	Prep time: 5 minutes	Slow-cook time: 10 hours
		Finish time: 5 minutes	Equipment: 6- to 8-quart slow cooker and cheesecloth

See the photo on page 2.

Staples, Sides, Beans, and Lentils

Bacon-Braised Greens, 7

Basic Slow-Cooked Beans, 12

Basic Slow-Cooked Lentils, 11

Big-Batch Caramelized Onions, 10

Basic Slow-Cooked Chickpeas, 13

Winter Tomato Sauce, 8

Bacon-Braised Greens

This recipe is inspired by the bacon-y, long-cooked hearty greens that you often find in the South. If you can't find thick-cut bacon, use 3 instead of 2 strips. The amount of hot sauce might seem like a lot, but by the time the greens are done cooking, the hot sauce has mixed with the greens' moisture and the whole thing has mellowed out considerably.

2 thick-cut bacon slices, chopped

2 bunches of kale (8 to 10 ounces each) or other hearty greens, such as mustard or collard, stemmed and chopped

1 tablespoon hot sauce, preferably a vinegary Louisiana-style sauce like Trappey's, Tabasco, or Louisiana Brand (Red Dot)

¼ teaspoon kosher salt

1. Place the bacon into a small dry skillet over medium heat. Cook, stirring occasionally, until the bacon is crisp and browned, about 8 minutes.

2. Put the crisp bacon and its rendered fat into a 5- to 8-quart slow cooker and add the greens, hot sauce, and salt. Stir to combine. (If your bunches of greens are generous and your slow cooker is on the small end of the range, you may have to pack the greens in. That's okay; they will shrink.) Cover and cook on LOW until the greens are very tender and mellow, 3 to 4 hours. A larger slow cooker will cook the greens more quickly than a smaller one.

Holds well on warm through step 2 for up to about 30 minutes	Prep time: 10 minutes	Slow-cook time: 3 to 4 hours	Equipment: 5- to 8-quart slow cooker

Winter Tomato Sauce

MAKES ABOUT 3½ CUPS

This is a slow-cooker adaptation of Marcella Hazan's famous 3-ingredient marinara sauce. The butter makes the sauce plush. Good-quality canned tomatoes are a useful pantry staple year-round but especially in winter when fresh tomatoes seem a lifetime away.

Two 28-ounce cans whole tomatoes

8 tablespoons (1 stick) unsalted butter, cut into pieces

2 medium yellow or red onions, halved

2 teaspoons kosher salt, plus more to taste

1. Combine all the ingredients in a 5- to 8-quart slow cooker, breaking up and crushing the tomatoes with your hands. Cover and cook on HIGH for 1 hour.

2. Uncover the slow cooker, stir well, reduce the heat to LOW, and then set the lid ajar by about 1 inch to allow the sauce to reduce. Cook until thick and delicious, about 5 hours, stirring occasionally if you can.

3. Remove and discard the onions. Taste and add more salt if desired. Cool the sauce, then store in an airtight container in the refrigerator for up to 1 week or in the freezer for up to 6 months.

ALL-DAY	Holds well on warm through steps 1 or 2 for up to 3 hours	Prep time: 5 minutes	Slow-cook time: 6 hours
		Finish time: 5 minutes	Equipment: 5- to 8-quart slow cooker

See the photo on page 6.

4 Ways to Turn Tomato Sauce into Dinner

SHAKSHUKA: In a large skillet, sauté sliced red bell peppers and onions in olive oil until soft, season with salt and red pepper flakes, then add the sauce and let it bubble. Crack eggs into the pan, cover, and cook until the eggs are just set, about 3 minutes. Serve with bread for mopping up the sauce.

POLENTA MARINARA: Stir the tomato sauce into warm Easy, Perfect Polenta (page 9) or instant polenta and top with grated Parmesan cheese and fresh herbs.

WEEKNIGHT SKILLET PIZZA: Buy a round of raw pizza dough at your local pizza parlor or at the supermarket. Roll out the crust and fit it into a large preheated cast-iron skillet. Top with tomato sauce and mozzarella plus your favorite toppings and bake at 425°F until the crust is cooked through and browned on the edges.

TOMATO-BRAISED CHICKEN: Sear chicken thighs in a skillet with diced pancetta, then pour in a little white wine and some tomato sauce, just enough to come halfway up the chicken thighs. Simmer until the chicken is cooked through, about 20 minutes, then add a handful of spinach and stir until wilted.

Easy, Perfect Polenta

A long, slow cooking time makes polenta glossy, creamy, and tender. Check out page 107 for one idea for how to turn it into a full meal on a weeknight. Here, the polenta cooks in salted water that's enriched with a little butter for flavor and texture—that way you can really taste the corn and the dish is satisfying but not at all heavy. If you usually prefer polenta cooked in milk, stir in a few spoonfuls of heavy cream at the end.

1½ cups polenta (not instant or quick-cooking)

2 tablespoons unsalted butter, cut into bits

2 teaspoons kosher salt

1. Combine all the ingredients in a 4- to 7-quart slow cooker and stir in 6½ cups water. Cover and cook on LOW until the polenta is creamy and tender, about 6 hours.

2. Stir well and then let the polenta sit with the lid off for about 2 minutes. Stir again. The polenta will thicken slightly. Add warm water by the spoonful if the polenta is looking too thick for your taste. (Keep in mind that the polenta will continue to firm up as it cools.)

All-DAY			
Holds well on warm through step 1 for up to 3 hours	Prep time: 5 minutes	Slow-cook time: 6 hours	Equipment: 4- to 7-quart slow cooker

Big-Batch Caramelized Onions

This idea is adapted from a Cook's Illustrated recipe; Cook's Illustrated is very big on microwaving ingredients before putting them into a slow cooker. In general, I prefer sautéing on the stovetop before slow cooking, because you get browning and, I think, better flavor. But in this case, the microwave step is a genius move. It allows the onions to give off a bunch of liquid all at once before you cook them, which in turn helps them acquire a soft, jammy texture in the slow cooker.

4 to 5 pounds yellow or red onions (this can range from 5 very large onions to 15 very small onions), halved and thinly sliced (about 16 cups)

Kosher salt

1 tablespoon vegetable oil

4 tablespoons (½ stick) unsalted butter, cut into bits

1 large fresh thyme sprig

2 teaspoons balsamic vinegar

1. Mound the sliced onions in a large microwave-safe bowl. Toss them with a generous pinch of salt and the oil. Microwave for 15 minutes on high, stirring every 5 minutes. The onions will shrink and give off liquid.

2. Drain all the liquid from the onions and put them into a 6- to 8-quart slow cooker. Add the butter, thyme, and 2 teaspoons salt and toss to evenly combine. Cover and cook on HIGH until the onions are very deeply golden, soft, and sweet, about 9 hours, stirring at least twice, especially around the edges.

3. Stir the onions well, add the vinegar, and set the lid ajar by about 2 inches so any moisture can reduce. Cook on HIGH until soft, sweet, and jammy, about 30 more minutes. Cool the onions, then store in an airtight container in the refrigerator for up to 1 week or in the freezer for up to 6 months.

Holds well on warm through step 2 for up to 2 hours	Prep time: 20 minutes	Slow-cook time: 9 hours 30 minutes	Equipment: 6- to 8-quart slow cooker

See the photo on page 6.

Basic Slow-Cooked Lentils

Beluga and green French lentils are especially useful because when cooked they get tender but still hold their shape and have a firm bite that's satisfying in salads or sautés. One of my favorite packed lunches is a big bowl of lentils (warm or straight from the fridge), good canned tuna packed in olive oil, arugula or baby kale, thinly sliced red onion, and capers. Add balsamic or sherry vinegar (or lemon juice) and a little bit of oil and you're done. Or try the Lentil Salad with Smoked Trout and Avocado (page 85).

1 pound beluga lentils, green French lentils, or, in a pinch, regular brown lentils (but not red lentils, which will disintegrate)

1 teaspoon kosher salt

1. Combine the lentils, salt, and 6 cups water in a 4- to 6-quart slow cooker and cook on LOW until the lentils are tender but still hold their shape, about 3 hours.

2. Drain. Let the lentils cool and then store them in an airtight container in the refrigerator for up to 5 days or in the freezer for up to 6 months.

| Does not hold well on warm | Prep time: 5 minutes | Slow-cook time: 3 hours | Equipment: 4- to 6-quart slow cooker |

See the photo on page 6.

4 Ways to Turn Caramelized Onions into Dinner

ONION AND OLIVE TART: Defrost puff pastry, roll it out, prick it all over with a fork, and brush it with olive oil. Put it on a baking sheet and top with a generous handful of caramelized onions, good-quality anchovies, pitted olives, and thyme leaves. Bake at 400°F until golden and cooked through, about 30 minutes, then scatter the top with crumbled goat cheese.

QUICK (SLOW) ONION SOUP: Combine caramelized onions and 24-Hour Beef Stock (page 3) and simmer until warmed through, about 10 minutes.

FLATBREADS WITH FIG AND BLUE CHEESE: Top store-bought flatbreads with some caramelized onions, sliced dried figs, and crumbled blue cheese. Broil until warm and toasty, 3 to 5 minutes.

BACON-ONION FRITTATA: Crisp chopped bacon in a skillet and stir in a handful of caramelized onions. Add 8 beaten eggs and ½ cup milk, and season with salt. Bake at 350°F until set in the center, about 18 minutes.

Basic Slow-Cooked Beans

I love this slow-cooker technique because you don't have to remember to soak the beans. However, if you prefer to soak you certainly can; it will cut the cook time roughly in half, to 4 to 5 hours. I wish I could give a more precise cooking time than 8 to 11 hours here. I have found that medium-size beans are generally tender at about 9 hours, but I have had batches that took up to 11 hours. The truth is that beans cook at very different rates depending on how old they are—and even if you've just bought the bag, it may have been sitting on the shelf for quite some time. Given those differences, plus the fact that smaller beans will generally cook more quickly than larger ones, and the fact that all slow cookers work differently, I can only give this estimate. Do it once and you'll have a better idea of how your slow cooker performs. The good news is that if the beans overcook a bit you can mix them with olive oil and herbs and make a dip or sandwich spread.

1 pound dried cannellini, cranberry, or black beans or black-eyed peas or other similar-size dried bean

1 teaspoon kosher salt

1. Put the beans into a large saucepan and cover them with water by at least 1 inch. Bring to a boil over high heat, then lower the heat and simmer for 10 minutes.

2. Drain the beans and put them into the slow cooker. Add the salt and 6 cups water and cook on LOW until tender, 8 to 11 hours. Generally, smaller beans (such as black-eyed peas) will cook faster than larger beans (such as cannellini), and older beans will cook slower than newer beans.

3. Drain. Let the beans cool and then store them in an airtight container in the refrigerator for up to 5 days or in the freezer for up to 6 months.

Good to know: Don't skip the boiling step before slow cooking the beans—some beans, particularly kidney beans, have a toxin that causes stomach upset and it's only deactivated by boiling.

ALL-DAY	Holds well on warm through step 2 for up to about 1 hour	Prep time: 10 minutes	Slow-cook time: 8 to 11 hours	Equipment: 4- to 6-quart slow cooker

See the photo on page 6.

Basic Slow-Cooked Chickpeas

Chickpeas need higher heat than other dried beans to become tender. They're also sturdier in general, so they can handle holding on warm better than other beans.

1 pound dried chickpeas
1 teaspoon kosher salt

1. Put the chickpeas into a large saucepan and cover them with water by at least 1 inch. Bring to a boil over high heat, then lower the heat and simmer for 10 minutes.

2. Drain the chickpeas and put them into the slow cooker. Add the salt and 6 cups water and cook on HIGH until tender, 8 to 9 hours.

3. Drain. Let the chickpeas cool and then store them in an airtight container in the refrigerator for up to 5 days or in the freezer for up to 6 months.

ALL-DAY	Holds well on warm through step 2 for up to about 2 hours	Prep time: 10 minutes	Slow-cook time: 8 to 9 hours	Equipment: 4- to 6-quart slow cooker

See the photo on page 6.

4 Ways to Turn Beans into Dinner

INDIAN-SPICED BEANS WITH YOGURT: Sauté a chopped onion and a small handful of chopped fresh ginger and garlic in vegetable oil. Season with salt and add a spoonful of curry powder or garam masala. Add some cooked lentils, beans, or chickpeas and cook until warmed through, about 5 minutes. Top with cilantro, yogurt, and scallions.

BEAN AND SAUSAGE SKILLET: Brown whole sausages in hot olive oil in a cast-iron skillet. Add some cooked beans, lentils, or chickpeas along with chopped fresh rosemary and salt. Cover and cook until the sausages are cooked through, about 10 minutes. Stir in olives or capers.

BEAN TACOS: Melt some butter in a skillet, then add a chopped garlic clove and some cooked beans and sauté until warmed through, about 5 minutes. Season with red pepper flakes and salt. Coarsely mash the beans with a fork and spoon into warm tortillas. Top with pickled or raw sliced red onion, cilantro, and crumbled *queso fresco*.

BEAN AND SPINACH SOUP: Cook pancetta or bacon until crisp, then add a chopped onion and chopped garlic clove and cook until soft. Add Classic Chicken Stock (page 5) or Parmesan-Garlic Broth (page 4), then cooked lentils, beans, or chickpeas. Simmer until hot. Season with salt and stir in spinach until wilted. Top with grated Parmesan.

Grains

For ideas on how to make these steamed grains into almost instant weeknight meals, see the five no-cook grain-bowl recipes starting on page 80.

Spelt, 16

Black rice, 15

Barley, 17

Brown rice, 16

Farro, 15

Steamed Farro

2 cups pearled farro (about 14 ounces), well rinsed under cold running water and drained in a fine-mesh strainer

2 cups boiling water

1 tablespoon olive or canola oil

¾ teaspoon kosher salt

1. Combine all the ingredients in a 5- to 7-quart slow cooker. Press a sheet of foil on top of the mixture so that the foil is touching the water and the entire mixture is shielded. (This is to keep the grains on top from drying out.) Cover and cook on HIGH until the farro is tender and the water is absorbed, 1 hour 30 minutes.

2. Remove the farro from the slow cooker immediately and fluff with a fork. Let the farro cool and then store it in an airtight container in the refrigerator for up to 5 days or in the freezer for up to 6 months.

Does not hold well on warm	Prep time: 5 minutes	Slow-cook time: 1 hour 30 minutes	Equipment: 5- to 7-quart slow cooker

Steamed Black Rice

2 cups black rice (about 14 ounces)

1 tablespoon olive or canola oil

¾ teaspoon kosher salt

1. Stir together all the ingredients in the slow cooker, add 2¼ cups cool water, and cook on HIGH until the rice is just tender and the water is absorbed, about 1 hour 30 minutes.

2. Remove the rice from the slow cooker immediately and fluff with a fork. Let the rice cool and then store it in an airtight container in the refrigerator for up to 5 days or in the freezer for up to 6 months.

Does not hold well on warm	Prep time: 5 minutes	Slow-cook time: 1 hour 30 minutes	Equipment: 5- to 7-quart slow cooker

Steamed Brown Rice

2 cups long- or medium-grain brown rice (about 13 ounces), such as brown basmati or jasmine

2¾ cups boiling water

1 tablespoon olive or canola oil

¾ teaspoon kosher salt

1. Combine all the ingredients in a 5- to 7-quart slow cooker. Press a sheet of foil on top of the mixture so that the foil is touching the water and the entire mixture is shielded. (This is to keep the grains on top from drying out.) Cover and cook on HIGH until the rice is just tender and the water is absorbed, 1 hour 30 minutes to 2 hours.

2. Remove the rice from the slow cooker immediately and fluff with a fork. Let the rice cool and then store it in an airtight container in the refrigerator for up to 5 days or in the freezer for up to 6 months.

Does not hold well on warm	Prep time: 5 minutes	Slow-cook time: 1 hour 30 minutes to 2 hours	Equipment: 5- to 7-quart slow cooker

See the photo on page 14.

Steamed Spelt

2 cups whole spelt berries (about 14.5 ounces), rinsed well under cold running water and drained in a fine-mesh strainer

2 cups boiling water

1 tablespoon olive or canola oil

¾ teaspoon kosher salt

1. Combine all the ingredients in a 5- to 7-quart slow cooker. Press a sheet of foil on top of the mixture so that the foil is touching the water and the entire mixture is shielded. (This is to keep the grains on top from drying out.) Cover and cook on HIGH until the spelt is tender and the water is absorbed, 4 hours to 4 hours 30 minutes.

2. Remove the spelt from the slow cooker immediately and fluff with a fork. Let the spelt cool and then store it in an airtight container in the refrigerator for up to 5 days or in the freezer for up to 6 months.

Does not hold well on warm	Prep time: 5 minutes	Slow-cook time: 4 hours to 4 hours 30 minutes	Equipment: 5- to 7-quart slow cooker

See the photo on page 14.

Steamed Barley

2 cups pearled barley (about 14 ounces), rinsed well under cold running water and drained in a fine-mesh strainer

1¾ cups boiling water

1 tablespoon olive or canola oil

¾ teaspoon kosher salt

1. Combine all the ingredients in a 5- to 7-quart slow cooker. Press a sheet of foil on top of the mixture so that the foil is touching the water and the entire mixture is shielded. (This is to keep the grains on top from drying out.) Cover and cook on HIGH until the barley is tender and the water is absorbed, 1 hour 30 minutes.

2. Remove the barley from the slow cooker immediately and fluff with a fork. Let the barley cool and then store it in an airtight container in the refrigerator for up to 5 days or in the freezer for up to 6 months.

Does not hold well on warm	Prep time: 5 minutes	Slow-cook time: 1 hour 30 minutes	Equipment: 5- to 7-quart slow cooker

See the photo on page 14.

JAM, LEFT TO RIGHT: Strawberry-Vanilla Jam
with Lime Zest, Peach–Orange Blossom Jam,
and Bittersweet Grapefruit-Ginger Marmalade

Preserves and Condiments

Traditionally, many condiments, jams, and spreads are cooked gently on the stovetop, so it's natural to adapt them to the slow cooker. You'll notice that most of these recipes call for removing or setting the lid ajar at the end—that's so the condiments thicken to a spreadable consistency, just as they do when they reduce on the stovetop. The exceptions are the jams and marmalade, which are set with pectin, a natural gelling agent that's found in fruit.

*All-day recipes: These recipes can cook or hold on warm unattended for 8 hours or more.

Strawberry-Vanilla Jam with Lime Zest

MAKES SIX 8-OUNCE JARS (ABOUT 6 CUPS)

Strawberries and vanilla bean both have a floral sweetness, and they marry together beautifully. A bit of lime zest stirred in at the end adds a little zip. I generally prefer to freeze jam rather than can it, but you can go either way, of course.

3 pounds ripe strawberries (about 4 pints), hulled and quartered

1 vanilla bean or 2 teaspoons pure vanilla extract

¾ cup sugar

2 tablespoons honey

Finely grated zest and juice of 1 lime

Generous pinch of kosher salt

2 tablespoons (about .5 ounce) low-sugar pectin, such as Ball RealFruit Low or No-Sugar Needed Pectin

1. Place the strawberries in a 5- to 8-quart slow cooker and coarsely mash them with your hands or a potato masher. Using a sharp paring knife, halve the vanilla bean lengthwise, scrape out the seeds, and add the bean halves and seeds to the slow cooker. Add the sugar, honey, lime juice, and salt and stir well to combine. Cover and cook on **HIGH** for 1 hour 30 minutes.

2. Whisk in the pectin and the lime zest, whisking very well for 30 seconds or so. Cover and cook for 5 minutes on **HIGH**.

3. Remove and discard the vanilla bean halves. To can the jam, follow the correct canning process to make shelf-stable preserves. To freeze or refrigerate it, ladle the jam into six 8-ounce jars, leaving about a half inch of headspace, and let cool before sealing. Store the jam in the refrigerator for up to 1 month or in the freezer for up to 6 months.

Good to know: Freshpreserving.com has reliable canning directions.

Holds well on warm for up to 1 hour through step 1. Be sure to turn the heat back up to high to let it warm up before adding the pectin.	Prep time: 20 minutes	Slow-cook time: 1 hour 30 minutes
	Finish time: 10 minutes	Equipment: 5- to 8-quart slow cooker

See the photo on page 18.

Peach-Orange Blossom Jam

MAKES EIGHT 8-OUNCE JARS (ABOUT 8 CUPS)

If you happen to have a bunch of ripe (or even overripe) summer peaches, this is a wonderful way to preserve them. Or you could use frozen peaches—I've had good luck with Whole Foods' 365 brand—which would mean you get to skip step 1.

4 pounds fresh ripe peaches (about 11 medium) or frozen peach slices, thawed and drained

1 cup sugar

Juice of 1 lemon

4 teaspoons finely grated orange zest

Pinch of kosher salt

3 tablespoons (about .75 ounce) low-sugar pectin, such as Ball RealFruit Low or No-Sugar Needed Pectin

2 teaspoons orange blossom water

1. If using fresh peaches, bring a large pot of water to a rolling boil. Fill a large bowl with ice water and set aside. On the bottom of each peach, using a paring knife, cut through the skin to make an X. Working with 3 or 4 peaches at a time, drop the peaches into the boiling water for 30 seconds to 1 minute. Remove the peaches with a slotted spoon and drop them into the ice water. Repeat with the remaining peaches. Starting from the flaps of skin where you scored the bottom of the peaches, pull the skins from the peaches. They should peel easily. Halve the peaches, discard the pits, and slice the peach halves into about 8 slices each.

2. Combine the peach slices, sugar, lemon juice, 2 teaspoons of the orange zest, and the salt in a 5- to 8-quart slow cooker and cook on **HIGH** for 2 hours.

3. Uncover and coarsely mash the peaches with a potato masher (or use an immersion blender to puree the peaches for a smoother jam). Whisk in the pectin, whisk well for about 30 seconds, cover, and cook on **HIGH** for 5 minutes.

4. Uncover, turn off the heat, and stir in the remaining 2 teaspoons orange zest and the orange blossom water. To can the jam, follow the correct canning process to make shelf-stable preserves. To freeze or refrigerate it, ladle the jam into eight 8-ounce jars, leaving about a half inch of headspace, and let cool before sealing. Store the jam in the refrigerator for up to 1 month or in the freezer for up to 6 months.

Good to know: Freshpreserving.com has reliable canning directions.

Holds well on warm through step 2 for up to 1 hour. Be sure to turn the heat back up to high to let it warm up before adding the pectin.	Prep time: 20 minutes with fresh peaches, 5 minutes with frozen	Slow-cook time: 2 hours
	Finish time: 10 minutes	Equipment: 5- to 8-quart slow cooker

See the photo on page 18.

Bittersweet Grapefruit-Ginger Marmalade

MAKES NINE 8-OUNCE JARS (ABOUT 9 CUPS)

This spread showcases the punchy, assertive flavors of grapefruit zest and ginger. Try it spooned into yogurt or on ricotta toast.

4 pounds grapefruit (about 4 large or 5 medium)

One 4-inch ginger knob, peeled and coarsely chopped (about ¼ cup)

4 cups sugar

1½ cups grapefruit juice

Pinch of kosher salt

½ cup (2.5 ounces) pectin, such as Ball RealFruit Classic Pectin

1. Using a vegetable peeler, peel the zest from the grapefruit in strips. Put the zest into a food processor with the ginger and process until finely chopped. Scrape the mixture into a 5- to 8-quart slow cooker. Slice off the tops and bottoms from the grapefruit so that they sit flat on your cutting board. Following the curve of the fruit, cut off all the peel and bitter white pith from the grapefruit and discard. Your grapefruit are now naked. Working over the slow cooker to catch the juice, cut between the grapefruit membranes to release the segments into the slow cooker. Discard the membranes and any seeds. Using your hands, crush and squeeze the grapefruit segments until the flesh is broken into small pieces. Stir in the sugar, grapefruit juice, salt, and 2 cups water. Cover and cook on LOW for 9 hours.

2. Increase the heat to HIGH and cook for 15 minutes. Whisk in the pectin. Whisk well for about 30 seconds, then cover and cook on HIGH for 5 minutes.

3. Uncover and stir well. To can the marmalade, follow the correct canning process to make shelf-stable preserves. To freeze or refrigerate it, ladle the marmalade into nine 8-ounce jars, leaving about a half inch of headspace, and let cool before sealing. Store the marmalade in the refrigerator for up to 1 month or in the freezer for up to 6 months.

Good to know: *Freshpreserving.com has reliable canning directions.*

ALL-DAY	Holds well on warm through step 1 for up to 2 hours	Prep time: 40 minutes	Slow-cook time: 9 hours
		Finish time: 20 minutes	Equipment: 5- to 8-quart slow cooker

See the photo on page 18.

Gingery Cranberry Chutney

This chutney would be right at home on the Thanksgiving table, but I also like having it around to sauce pork chops, duck breast, or steak. It makes a really nice topping for ricotta toast or yogurt, too. I stir in a second bit of ginger at the very end for a superfresh pop of ginger flavor that hasn't been mellowed by cooking.

24 ounces fresh cranberries or two 12-ounce bags frozen cranberries, thawed

1½ cups packed light brown sugar

1 tablespoon balsamic vinegar

1 teaspoon red pepper flakes

½ teaspoon ground cinnamon

Kosher salt

¼ cup grated ginger (from about a peeled 4-inch ginger knob)

1. Combine the cranberries, sugar, vinegar, red pepper flakes, cinnamon, and ½ teaspoon salt in a 5- to 8-quart slow cooker. (If you want to use a 4-quart slow cooker, it will work, but the cooking times will be longer.) Stir in all but 2 teaspoons of the ginger. Cover and cook on HIGH for 1 hour 30 minutes.

2. Uncover the slow cooker and stir well, especially around the edges. Set the lid ajar by about 2 inches to let steam escape and cook on HIGH for about 1 hour more, until many of the cranberries have popped and the sauce is slightly thickened, stirring about every 15 minutes to prevent burning around the edges.

3. Stir in the remaining 2 teaspoons ginger. Let the sauce cool slightly, then taste and add more salt if necessary. Ladle the chutney into an airtight container and let cool completely before sealing. Store the chutney in the refrigerator for up to 2 weeks or in the freezer for up to 6 months.

Holds well on warm through step 1 for up to 2 hours	Prep time: 5 minutes	Slow-cook time: 2 hours 30 minutes
	Finish time: Occasional stirring for the last hour	Equipment: 5- to 8-quart slow cooker

See the photo on page 25.

Spiced Pumpkin Butter

I'm not a fan of the weirdly pumpkin-free pumpkin spice craze that descends every fall. But I am a fan of actual pumpkin with spices. Here, the pumpkin puree is cooked very slowly so that all its water evaporates, leaving behind a dense, sweet condiment that's pretty wonderful spread on toast or waffles, stirred into yogurt, or even layered in a savory-sweet grilled cheese. (Fruit "butter" gets its name from its silky spreadable texture, not because it actually contains any butter.) It also makes your house smell like you've been baking pumpkin pie all day. A jar makes a welcome dinner party gift around the holidays. The ¾ cup maple syrup makes a lightly sweet spread, which I prefer, but you can increase it to 1 cup for a sweeter result.

¾ cup to 1 cup pure maple syrup

½ cup unsweetened applesauce

1 teaspoon ground cinnamon

½ teaspoon ground cardamom

½ teaspoon ground ginger

¼ teaspoon kosher salt

Two 15-ounce cans pure pumpkin puree (not pumpkin pie mix)

Juice of ¼ small lemon

1. Combine the maple syrup, applesauce, cinnamon, cardamom, ginger, salt, and pumpkin puree in a 4- to 6-quart slow cooker. Stir well, cover, and cook on **HIGH** for 1 hour 30 minutes.

2. Remove the lid and cook on **HIGH** for about 3 hours, stirring at least once an hour to prevent scorching, especially around the edges. (The larger your slow cooker, the shorter the cook time. If you're using a 4-quart slow cooker, you may need to cook for an additional 30 minutes or so.) The butter is done when it is slightly darkened in color and has thickened and reduced. It should be sweet, smooth, and dense because much of the water has evaporated.

3. Squeeze in the lemon juice. Spoon the butter into seven 4-ounce jars or other containers and let cool before sealing. Store the butter in the refrigerator for up to 2 weeks or in the freezer for up to 6 months.

Good to know: Pumpkin butter is not suitable for home canning (because of pumpkins' low acidity), so freezing is the only preserving option here.

Holds well on warm through step 1 for up to 2 hours	Prep time: 5 minutes	Slow-cook time: About 4 hours 30 minutes
	Finish time: Occasional stirring for the last 3 hours	Equipment: 4- to 6-quart slow cooker

Spiced Pumpkin Butter on toast and
Gingery Cranberry Chutney, 23, with yogurt

Rosemary-Honey Applesauce

A firm, sweet-tart apple is best here. I like Honeycrisp or Braeburn; feel free to use a mix of varieties.

5 pounds apples, peeled, cored, and roughly chopped

⅓ cup honey, plus more to taste

½ teaspoon kosher salt

3 large fresh rosemary sprigs

Juice of 1 lemon, plus more to taste

1. Combine all the ingredients in a 5- to 8-quart slow cooker and stir. Cover and cook on **HIGH** until the apples are very soft, about 5 hours, stirring once or twice if possible.

2. Remove the rosemary sprigs and mash the apples with a potato masher. Add more lemon juice or honey to taste. Ladle the applesauce into sealable containers and let cool completely before covering and refrigerating or freezing. Store the applesauce in the refrigerator for up to 2 weeks or in the freezer for up to 6 months.

ALL-DAY	Holds well on warm through step 1 for up to 3 hours	Prep time: 30 minutes	Slow-cook time: 5 hours
		Finish time: 10 minutes	Equipment: 5- to 8-quart slow cooker

Smoky Chipotle Ketchup

Heinz ketchup is perfect, and I wouldn't even try to improve on it. (And yes, I know it's full of sugar, and yes, that's probably why it's so good.) This recipe is a completely different beast: a superspicy and smoky condiment that's fantastic on lamb burgers or used as a glaze for meat loaf. You can add the amount of chipotles that suits you. I think a little less than half the can makes for a very spicy but not insane result.

One 28-ounce can tomato puree

½ cup honey

¼ cup tomato paste

1 tablespoon canola or vegetable oil

¼ teaspoon ground allspice

1½ teaspoons kosher salt, plus more if necessary

One 7-ounce can chipotle chiles in adobo sauce

1. Combine the tomato puree, honey, tomato paste, oil, allspice, and salt in a blender. Add a little less than half of the can of chipotles (both chiles and sauce) and blend until smooth. (Alternatively, add these ingredients directly to the slow cooker and blend with an immersion blender.) Taste and gradually add more chipotles if you'd like a spicier ketchup. Scrape the puree into a 5- to 6-quart slow cooker. Cover and cook on HIGH for 1 hour.

2. Set the lid ajar by about 2 inches and cook on HIGH until the ketchup is thickened and slightly darkened in color, about 3 more hours, stirring at least once an hour to prevent scorching, especially around the edges. (The larger the slow cooker, the less time it will take.) Taste and add more salt if necessary. Let cool and then store the sauce in an airtight container in the refrigerator for up to 2 weeks or in the freezer for up to 6 months.

Holds well on warm through step 1	Prep time: 10 minutes	Slow-cook time: About 4 hours
	Finish time: Occasional stirring for the last 3 hours	Equipment: 5- to 6-quart slow cooker

See the photo on page 29.

Brown Sugar-Bourbon Barbecue Sauce

This hits all the flavors you want from a classic barbecue sauce: sweet, spicy, tangy, and smoky. (You might be surprised how potent smoked paprika can be.) The bourbon adds a little sharpness and complexity.

4 garlic cloves, chopped

1 medium or large yellow or red onion, chopped

One 28-ounce can tomato puree

¼ cup plus 1½ teaspoons bourbon or whiskey

½ cup packed light brown sugar

¼ cup unsulphured molasses

1 tablespoon honey

2 teaspoons Dijon mustard

2 teaspoons red pepper flakes

2 teaspoons kosher salt, plus more if necessary

1 teaspoon smoked paprika

½ teaspoon ground cloves

1 teaspoon balsamic vinegar

1. Combine the garlic, onion, tomato puree, and ¼ cup of the bourbon in a blender and blend until smooth. Scrape the puree into a 5- to 8-quart slow cooker and add the sugar, molasses, honey, mustard, red pepper flakes, salt, paprika, and cloves. Stir well. Cover and cook on **HIGH** for 2 hours.

2. Remove the lid and cook on **HIGH**, uncovered, for 2 to 3 hours (the larger the slow cooker, the less time it will take), stirring at least once an hour to prevent scorching, especially around the edges. When it's done, the sauce will have darkened and thickened to a classic barbecue sauce consistency. Add the remaining 1½ teaspoons bourbon and the vinegar. Taste and add more salt if necessary. Let cool and then store the sauce in an airtight container in the refrigerator for up to 2 weeks or in the freezer for up to 6 months.

Holds well on warm through step 1	Prep time: 10 minutes	Slow-cook time: 4 to 5 hours
	Finish time: Occasional stirring for the last 2 to 3 hours	Equipment: 5- to 8-quart slow cooker

Brown Sugar–Bourbon Barbecue Sauce
and Smoky Chipotle Ketchup, 27

Crisp Chicken Wings with Spicy
Sichuan Caramel

Appetizers, Snacks, and Cocktails

The Parties chapter (page 155) is dedicated to dinner party recipes, but this section is also geared toward entertaining—occasions when you might need a crunchy snack or a plate of wings, a warm cheese dip or mulled wine. It's a bit of a hodgepodge, I know, but sometimes an occasion calls for chawan mushi and sometimes it calls for cheddar dip, and there's nothing wrong with that.

Crisp Chicken Wings with Spicy Sichuan Caramel

MAKES 4 SERVINGS

I'm a sucker for anything sweet-spicy, and these wings are very much both. Sichuan peppercorns add a floral, piney flavor. If you don't have a mortar and pestle to crush the peppercorns, you can just put them on a cutting board, lay a heavy skillet or pot over the top, and press down to crush.

3 pounds split chicken wings (mixed drumettes and wingettes)

2 tablespoons toasted sesame oil

3½ teaspoons kosher salt

¼ cup packed dark brown sugar

3 tablespoons Sichuan peppercorns, coarsely crushed in a mortar and pestle

3 tablespoons red pepper flakes, or more to taste

2 teaspoons white vinegar

2 tablespoons unsalted butter

Torn fresh cilantro leaves, for serving (optional)

1. Combine the wings, oil, and 2 teaspoons of the salt in a 5- to 8-quart slow cooker. Cover and cook until the wings register an internal temperature of at least 160°F when tested with an instant-read thermometer: on **LOW** for 3 hours (preferable, because the wings cook more evenly) or on **HIGH** for 1 hour 30 minutes to 2 hours. The wings will not get browned or crisp, but don't worry—you're going to take care of that in the broiler.

2. Preheat the broiler on high and position a rack about 6 inches below the heat source (if that's how your broiler is configured). Remove the wings from the slow cooker with tongs (leaving the drippings behind) and place them on a rimmed baking sheet. Broil the wings until the skin gets crisp and golden, flipping once, 5 to 10 minutes per side, 10 to 20 minutes total, depending on the strength of your broiler.

3. Meanwhile, in a small skillet, combine the sugar, peppercorns, red pepper flakes, and vinegar. Season the mixture with the remaining 1½ teaspoons salt and put it over medium-high heat, stirring occasionally. (The ingredients will liquefy into a savory caramel sauce.) Let the glaze just start to bubble, give it a stir, and then turn off the heat and stir in the butter until melted and smooth.

4. Pour the glaze into a large bowl that will fit all the wings comfortably. When the wings are crisp, immediately add them to the bowl and toss to evenly coat the wings in glaze. Top with cilantro, if desired, and serve right away.

Good to know: You can find Sichuan peppercorns at a Chinese market, the Mala Market (themalamarket.com), or on Amazon.

Holds on warm through step 1 for a maximum of 1 hour	Prep time: 5 minutes	Slow-cook time: 2 to 3 hours
	Finish time: 20 minutes	Equipment: 5- to 8-quart slow cooker

See the photo on page 30.

Mumbai Chaat Chex Mix

This updated Chex mix is inspired by a category of Indian snacks called chaat—*in particular bhel puri, an addictive snack mix that includes puffed rice and is popular in Mumbai. Chaat* masala *is a spice blend that's tart, hot, and a little sulfurous. If you can't find it, use all curry powder—it is not at all the same but will still be tasty. Most* chaat masala *has salt in it already, so you probably don't need to add more (though, as always, taste at the end, and if it's a little flat, add salt). If you're using unsalted curry powder, though, season the melted butter mixture with 1½ teaspoons kosher salt. The snack mix keeps well in a sealed container at room temperature for up to a week.*

3 cups Rice Chex cereal

3 cups Corn Chex cereal

2 cups puffed rice

1 cup unsalted cashews

1 cup unsweetened coconut flakes (chips)

8 tablespoons (1 stick) unsalted butter

2 tablespoons plus 1 teaspoon *chaat* masala

2 teaspoons red pepper flakes

1 teaspoon curry powder

1 teaspoon garlic powder

1 cup chopped dried mango

½ cup golden raisins

1. Combine the Chex, puffed rice, cashews, and coconut in a 5- to 8-quart slow cooker. In a small pot over low heat, melt the butter. Stir in the *chaat* masala, red pepper flakes, curry powder, and garlic powder. Pour the spiced, melted butter over the mixture in the slow cooker and toss well to coat evenly. Prop the lid partly open with a wooden spoon and cook on **HIGH** for 1 hour 30 minutes, stirring every 30 minutes to toast evenly.

2. Spread the warm cereal mix on a baking sheet. Toss in the dried mango and raisins. Let cool completely at room temperature. Store the mix in an airtight container at room temperature for up to a week.

Does not hold well on warm	Prep time: 10 minutes	Slow-cook time: 1 hour 30 minutes, with occasional stirring
	Finish time: 5 minutes plus cooling	Equipment: 5- to 8-quart slow cooker

See the photo on page 35.

Smoked Paprika and Maple Candied Nuts with Rosemary

Here's another variation on the sweet-savory theme. These lacquered nuts are most at home on a cheese plate, but they're also a wonderfully all-purpose snack and gift, especially around the holidays. I prefer to use unsalted nuts, so I can control the seasoning myself, but this will also work with salted nuts—just leave out the salt. Use any combination of nuts you like. I've done this with mixed nuts as well as just almonds and pecans, which is a very appealing combination.

1 pound mixed unsalted roasted nuts (about 2 cups)

¼ cup pure maple syrup

1½ tablespoons unsalted butter, melted

1 teaspoon kosher salt, plus more if necessary

1 teaspoon smoked paprika

½ teaspoon ground cinnamon

½ teaspoon red pepper flakes

1½ teaspoons minced fresh rosemary

1. Line a 5- to 8-quart slow cooker with a sheet of parchment paper, making sure it comes up the sides at least 2 inches (see page xxvi for a how-to). Combine the nuts, maple syrup, butter, salt, paprika, cinnamon, and red pepper flakes in the lined cooker and stir to combine evenly. Cover and cook on HIGH for 1 hour.

2. Uncover and stir well, concentrating on the edges against the insert walls, where burning is most likely. Set the lid ajar to leave a gap or vent of about 2 inches across and cook on HIGH until the maple syrup is reduced and sticky and the nuts smell toasty, 1 hour to 1 hour 30 minutes more (the larger your slow cooker, the shorter the cook time), stirring every 30 minutes to prevent burning around the edges.

3. Line a baking sheet with parchment paper. Grabbing the edges of the parchment liner in the slow cooker, lift the nuts out of the insert and carefully pour them out onto the prepared baking sheet. (The maple syrup is very hot, so be careful not to touch it.) Sprinkle the rosemary over the top and stir to combine and spread the nuts out evenly. Let cool completely at room temperature. Taste and add more salt if necessary. Store the nuts in an airtight container at room temperature for up to 5 days.

Does not hold well on warm	Prep time: 5 minutes	Slow-cook time: 2 hours to 2 hours 30 minutes, with occasional stirring
	Finish time: 5 minutes	Equipment: 5- to 8-quart slow cooker

TOP: Smoked Paprika and Maple Candied Nuts with Rosemary BOTTOM: Mumbai Chaat Chex Mix, 33

Chawan Mushi with Scallops and Shiitakes

Chawan mushi *is a silken, quivery steamed custard from Japan in which flavorful dashi stock is just barely held together with a few eggs. I love the delicate richness of scallops in this dish because their texture echoes the custard itself, but you can also use chopped shrimp. Food scientist Harold McGee says in his book* On Food and Cooking *that this dish is a combination of custard and soup—so the desired result is a very, very delicate custard with some lovely aromatic soup squidging out when you spoon into it.*

Two 4 × 3-inch pieces kombu seaweed or the equivalent in surface area (about .3 ounce)

⅓ cup (.176 ounce or 5 grams) dried bonito flakes

3 large eggs plus 1 egg yolk, lightly beaten

1 tablespoon mirin

1 teaspoon soy sauce, plus more for serving

Small pinch of kosher salt

2 shiitake mushrooms, caps only, thinly sliced

4 sea scallops, quartered

1 scallion, trimmed, light green and white parts thinly sliced, and dark green parts sliced and reserved for topping

1. Combine 2 cups cold water and the kombu in a small saucepan over medium-high heat. Bring the water just to a boil and remove the pan from the heat. Using tongs or a slotted spoon, remove and discard the kombu. Stir in the bonito flakes and let steep for 3 minutes. Line a fine-mesh strainer with cheesecloth and strain the broth into a bowl or container. You just made dashi! Put the dashi in the refrigerator to cool to at least room temperature. To speed this up, fill a large bowl with ice water and then set the bowl of dashi into the larger bowl before refrigerating. (You can make the dashi 1 day in advance and refrigerate it in an airtight container.)

2. In a medium bowl or large liquid measuring cup, combine the dashi with the beaten eggs and yolk, mirin, soy sauce, and salt and gently whisk. You want all the ingredients to combine evenly, but you don't want the mixture to get frothy.

3. Evenly divide the shiitakes, scallops, and scallion (white and light green parts) among four 1-cup (8-ounce) oven-safe glass or ceramic bowls or ramekins. Give the egg-dashi mixture one last gentle stir, then pour it into the ramekins, dividing it evenly. Blow on the surfaces of the custards to get rid of any little bubbles—it's not essential to get rid of them, but the finished custards look nicer with a smooth surface.

4. Pour 4 cups water into the slow cooker, to a depth of about 1 inch. Carefully place the ramekins into the slow cooker, making sure not to jostle any water into the ramekins. (The water should come about halfway

up the side of the bottom layer of the ramekins.) You might be able to set them all into the cooker in a single layer. If not, place 3 ramekins into the insert and then balance the remaining ramekin on top of the others. Place a double layer of paper towels over the top of the cooker to soak up condensation, leaving some overhang so that the paper towels don't fall onto the ramekins, and then close the lid on top of the paper towels (see page xx for a how-to). Cook on LOW until the custards are just set but still jiggly, 3 hours.

5. Turn off and uncover the slow cooker. Let the ramekins cool just enough for you to be able to reach in and pull them out. Serve the *chawan mushi* warm or chilled, topped with the reserved sliced scallion and a drizzle of soy sauce.

Good to know: Both kombu and bonito flakes are available on Amazon.

Does not hold well on warm	Prep time: 15 minutes, plus cooling the dashi	Slow-cook time: 3 hours	Finish time: 5 minutes
Equipment: 6-quart or larger slow cooker, cheesecloth, and four 1-cup (8-ounce) oven-safe glass or ceramic bowls or ramekins			

Recipe on
following page

Slow-Cooker Cheese Dips: Three Ideas

A slow cooker on warm can serve a dip at the perfect temperature for a couple of hours. You'll notice that the three cheese dips that follow have very different personalities, but they all contain cream cheese—that's to make sure they stay creamy and smooth, because melted cheese by itself can get grainy if kept warm. Leftover dip can be used as a sandwich spread or a pasta sauce (loosen it with pasta cooking water).

Sharp Cheddar and Peppadew Dip

MAKES ABOUT 5 CUPS

This party dip was inspired by pimento cheese. I love the sweet-tangy-spicy bite that the Peppadew peppers add, but you can certainly use chopped drained pimentos or roasted red peppers instead.

1 pound full-fat cream cheese (not cream cheese spread), at room temperature, cut into pieces

1 pound sharp cheddar, grated (about 4 cups)

8 ounces smoked gouda, rind removed, grated (about 2 cups)

1 cup drained, sliced Peppadew peppers, hot or mild (I prefer hot)

Red pepper flakes to taste

Toasted rustic bread strips and celery sticks, for serving

1. In a 4- to 6-quart slow cooker, stir together the cream cheese, cheddar cheese, and gouda. Cover and cook on LOW until most of the cheese is melted or almost melted, about 1 hour.

2. With a handheld electric mixer on high speed, beat the dip until it's creamy and uniform, about 1 minute. Reduce the heat to WARM and fold in the sliced peppers. Taste and season with red pepper flakes. Serve the dip from the slow cooker, still set on WARM, with toasted bread strips and celery for dipping. To store leftover dip, let it cool and then spoon it into a sealable container and refrigerate for up to 3 days.

Holds well on warm	Prep time: 10 minutes	Slow-cook time: 1 hour
	Finish time: 5 minutes	Equipment: 4- to 6-quart slow cooker

See the photo on page 39.

Garlicky Ricotta and Swiss Chard Dip

MAKES ABOUT 4 CUPS

This is like ravioli filling in dip form. Feel free to substitute collards, kale, or mustard greens for the chard.

1 bunch of Swiss chard (10 to 12 ounces), stemmed

16 ounces whole milk ricotta

8 ounces full-fat cream cheese (not cream cheese spread), at room temperature, cut into pieces

5 ounces Parmesan, finely grated (about 1½ cups)

4 garlic cloves, grated or minced

Juice of ½ lemon

1 teaspoon kosher salt, plus more to taste

Freshly ground black pepper

Endive leaves, baby carrots, radishes, and crackers, for serving

1. Bring a large pot of salted water to a boil. Drop in the chard, stir, and cook until just wilted, about 30 seconds. Drain, then run under cold water to stop the cooking. Thoroughly squeeze the greens dry and blot them on a paper towel or kitchen towel. Finely chop the greens and put them into a 4- to 6-quart slow cooker.

2. Add the ricotta, cream cheese, Parmesan, garlic, and lemon juice to the slow cooker and season with 1 teaspoon of salt and a generous amount of pepper. Stir to fully combine. Cover and cook on LOW until heated through and creamy, about 1 hour.

3. Reduce the heat to WARM, stir well, and taste for seasoning. Serve the dip from the slow cooker, with vegetables and crackers on the side. To store leftover dip, let it cool and then spoon it into a sealable container and refrigerate for up to 3 days.

| Holds well on warm | Prep time: 15 minutes | Slow-cook time: 1 hour | Equipment: 4- to 6-quart slow cooker |

Whipped Feta, Red Pepper, and Olive Dip

The sharp, briny flavors of feta and olives balance the richness of this creamy dip. Use the best feta you can lay your hands on and avoid those that are pre-crumbled.

11 ounces feta cheese, crumbled (about 2½ cups)

8 ounces full-fat cream cheese (not cream cheese spread), at room temperature, cut into pieces

1 cup crème fraîche or sour cream

2 tablespoons white wine

8 ounces jarred roasted red peppers, drained and chopped (about ⅔ cup)

⅓ cup sliced, pitted kalamata olives

1 teaspoon chopped fresh thyme

1 teaspoon red pepper flakes

Finely grated zest of ½ lemon

Pita chips, lavash, and assorted raw vegetables, for serving

1. Combine the feta and cream cheese in a 4- to 6-quart slow cooker. Use a handheld electric mixer to whip the feta and cream cheese until fluffy. Fold in the remaining ingredients except the chips and other dippers. Cover and cook on LOW until warmed through, about 1 hour.

2. Reduce the heat to WARM, stir well, and serve the dip from the slow cooker, with the bread and vegetables on the side.

Holds well on warm	Prep time: 15 minutes	Slow-cook time: 1 hour	Equipment: 4- to 6-quart slow cooker

Swedish Spiced White Wine with Almonds, 49

Mexican-Style Hot Chocolate, 50

Warm Cocktails: Eight Ideas

I love a warm cocktail in the wintertime. But when you keep a pot of spiced wine going on the stovetop, it's hard to keep the heat low enough so that the drink doesn't taste overly cooked and reduced. Also, alcohol burns off at about 170 °F, so if there's booze in that simmering pot, it's lost its potency.

Warm Triple-Citrus
Bourbon Punch, 47

Star Anise–Black Pepper
Hot Toddy, 45

Kentucky Nightcap, 51

The solution: Serve a cocktail in a slow cooker set on warm. It's the perfect temperature for sipping and for maintaining the alcohol's pop. In the unlikely event of leftovers, all these cocktails keep well in the fridge for at least a week, and can also be served chilled.

Star Anise-Black Pepper Hot Toddy

A hot toddy is made many different ways all around the world, but at its simplest, it's just hot water, lemon juice, honey, and booze—a cure for whatever ails you in the wintertime. This is a more festive, spiced version with a black tea base. English breakfast tea is especially good with the black pepper and star anise, but Earl Grey would be nice, too. Decaf versions of those teas are also totally fair game.

5 whole star anise

2 tablespoons whole black peppercorns

8 black tea bags

¾ cup honey, plus more to taste

2 cinnamon sticks

¾ cup freshly squeezed lemon juice, plus more to taste

2 cups rye whiskey

Lemon zest twists or lemon wheels, for serving

1. Put the star anise and peppercorns on a piece of cheesecloth and tie it into a bundle using kitchen twine or a thin strip of cheesecloth. (This makes it easier to serve without getting black peppercorns in your cup, but if you don't have cheesecloth, don't worry—just put the spices into the slow cooker.) Put the bundle into a 4- to 6-quart slow cooker. Add 10 cups water, the tea bags, honey, and cinnamon sticks. Cover and cook until the mixture tastes like good tea, about 2 hours on HIGH.

2. Reduce the heat to WARM. Pull out the tea bags, squeeze them over the pot to extract their liquid, and discard. Stir in the lemon juice and whiskey. Taste and add more honey or lemon juice if you feel it needs it. Serve from the slow cooker, still set on WARM, in mugs garnished with lemon zest twists or lemon wheels.

Holds well on warm	Prep time: 5 minutes	Slow-cook time: 2 hours
	Finish time: 5 minutes	Equipment: 4- to 6-quart slow cooker and cheesecloth

See the photo on page 45.

Warm Triple-Citrus Bourbon Punch

MAKES ABOUT 16 SERVINGS

This is for occasions when a real cocktail is called for: It's boozy and not too sweet, very citrusy. In the first step, you macerate orange peel and sugar to make an aromatic sugar called oleo saccharum, which is a fancy ye olde cocktail term for oily sugar. It punches up the orange flavor substantially.

Zest of 1 orange, removed in strips with a vegetable peeler

⅓ cup sugar

3 cups orange juice

1 cup grapefruit juice

1 cup freshly squeezed lemon juice, plus more if necessary

4 thin lemon slices

¼ cup honey, plus more to taste

10 whole cloves

4 cups bourbon

2 teaspoons orange curaçao (optional)

10 dashes of bitters, preferably orange bitters, but any kind will do

Orange wheels or twists, for serving (optional)

1. Combine the orange zest strips and the sugar in a zip-top bag. Close the bag and massage the mixture to combine. Let it sit at room temperature, massaging once or twice, for at least 5 hours. (You can also throw the bag into the fridge and let it sit for up to 2 weeks before using it.)

2. Scrape all the sugar and syrup off the orange zest strips and put the sugar and syrup into a 4- to 6-quart slow cooker. Discard the orange zest strips. Add 2½ cups water; the orange, grapefruit, and lemon juices; lemon slices; honey; and cloves. Cover and cook on HIGH until hot, 1 to 2 hours.

3. Reduce the heat to WARM and pour in the bourbon, curaçao (if desired), and bitters. Stir to combine and taste. Add more honey and/or water if the cocktail is too acidic for you or more lemon juice if you'd like it tangier. Serve from the slow cooker, still set on WARM, and if desired, garnish with orange wheels or twists.

Holds well on warm	Prep time: 5 minutes plus 6 hours macerating	Slow-cook time: 1 to 2 hours
	Finish time: 5 minutes	Equipment: 4- to 6-quart slow cooker

See the photo on page 45.

Coconut-Almond Tiki Coffee

The combination of creamy coconut and strong coffee with light and dark rum and almond liqueur is just outrageously good. If you want to serve this at a cocktail party, don't add the sugar at first; taste and see if you think it's needed. You might want to add just a little or let your friends add it to their mugs to taste. Or you could take this all the way into dessert land: Add the sugar and top with the whipped cream and coconut and/or almonds. Keep in mind that you can always use decaf coffee if you like; it won't affect the flavor.

6 cups strong brewed hot coffee

One 13.6-ounce can unsweetened coconut cream (not cream of coconut)

2 cups gold (amber) rum

1 cup dark rum

1½ cups amaretto

¼ cup sugar, plus more to taste (optional)

Whipped cream and sliced almonds and/or toasted unsweetened coconut flakes (optional)

Combine 1 cup of the hot coffee and the coconut cream in a blender and blend until the mixture is very smooth. Pour the mixture into a 4- to 6-quart slow cooker and add the rest of the hot coffee, the gold and dark rums, and the amaretto. If you would like to take this in the direction of an after-dinner dessert cocktail, add the sugar and taste to see if you want to add more. Set the slow cooker on WARM and serve the cocktail from the cooker. Top each serving with whipped cream and almonds or coconut, if desired.

Holds well on warm	Prep time: 10 minutes	Slow-cook time: Ready immediately; serve on warm	Equipment: 4- to 6-quart slow cooker

Swedish Spiced White Wine with Almonds

This is adapted from a Marcus Samuelsson recipe that I worked on at Food & Wine—*it's aromatic with cardamom, ginger, and orange and makes a refreshing change from more common (and, let's be honest, kind of dull) mulled red wine. The slivered almonds give a gentle flavor and crunch.*

1 tablespoon green cardamom pods

4 cinnamon sticks

One 2-inch ginger knob, peeled and sliced into thin planks

12 whole cloves

1 vanilla bean or 2 teaspoons pure vanilla extract

Two 3-inch strips orange zest, removed with a vegetable peeler

1½ cups sugar

Two 750-ml bottles dry white wine

1 cup dry rosé

1 cup vodka

½ cup slivered blanched almonds

1. Put the cardamom, cinnamon, ginger, and cloves on a piece of cheesecloth and tie it into a bundle using kitchen twine or a thin strip of cheesecloth. Put the bundle into a 4- to 6-quart slow cooker. Using a sharp paring knife, halve the vanilla bean lengthwise, scrape out the seeds, and add the bean halves and seeds to the slow cooker. Add the remaining ingredients and stir to combine. Set the slow cooker on LOW and cook for 30 minutes, then reduce the heat to WARM and cook for another 30 minutes to infuse the aromatics into the wine and warm the cocktail through.

2. Uncover, remove and discard the cheesecloth bundle, vanilla bean halves, and zest strips with a slotted spoon, and serve from the slow cooker with the setting still on WARM.

Holds well on warm	Prep time: 20 minutes	Slow-cook time: 1 hour
	Finish time: 5 minutes	Equipment: 4- to 6-quart slow cooker and cheesecloth

See the photo on page 44.

Mexican-Style Hot Chocolate

Traditional Mexican hot chocolate is more complex and aromatic than its American counterpart. This big-batch, slow-cooker version is flavored with vanilla, almond, warm spices like cinnamon, and a little bit of cayenne. You can sometimes find discs of prespiced Mexican chocolate at the grocery store that are designed for making hot cocoa, but I prefer to control the spicing and sugar myself. The only thing this is missing is the frothy top that's usually created with a special wooden whisk called a molinillo. *If you want to re-create that texture, carefully froth the hot chocolate with an immersion blender set in the slow cooker before serving.*

8 cups whole milk

14 ounces dark or bittersweet (about 70% cacao) chocolate, finely chopped (about 3 cups)

½ cup packed light brown sugar, plus more to taste

3 cinnamon sticks

Generous pinch of kosher salt

1 tablespoon pure vanilla extract

1 to 2 teaspoons almond extract, to taste

½ teaspoon freshly grated nutmeg

Pinch of cayenne, plus more for topping

Whipped cream and cocoa powder, for topping (both optional)

Mezcal or tequila, 1.5 ounces per serving (3 tablespoons), for spiking (optional)

1. Combine the milk, chocolate, sugar, cinnamon sticks, and salt in a 4- to 6-quart slow cooker. Whisk well, then cover and cook on LOW heat until the chocolate is melted, about 1 hour. Whisk vigorously until the mixture is smooth.

2. Reduce the heat to WARM and stir in the vanilla and almond extracts, nutmeg, and cayenne. Taste and whisk in a little more sugar if you would prefer it sweeter. Serve from the slow cooker, still set on WARM, and if desired, top each mug with whipped cream, a light dusting of cocoa, and cayenne. Spike with mezcal if you'd like.

Good to know: You can make the hot chocolate ahead through step 1 and then refrigerate it for up to 3 days. Pour it into the slow cooker and reheat on WARM *until it's warmed through, about 1 hour. Whisk to smooth it out and proceed with step 2.*

Holds well on warm	Prep time: 10 minutes	Slow-cook time: 1 hour to 1 hour 30 minutes
	Finish time: 5 minutes	Equipment: 4- to 6-quart slow cooker

See the photo on page 44.

Kentucky Nightcap

Fort Defiance in Red Hook, Brooklyn, is everything you want a neighborhood restaurant to be—it's comfortable and friendly; serves a great burger, deviled eggs, and oysters; and makes delicious cocktails. In the winter I always get the Kentucky Nightcap after dinner. It's soothing and so tasty: barely sweet steamed milk and bourbon, almost like a warm bourbon milk punch. This is my humble re-creation, with vanilla bean for extra deliciousness. (For this, it's really worth it to get a vanilla bean rather than using extract.) Put out a slow cooker filled with this cocktail at the end of a dinner party and watch everyone get reeeeeally relaxed.

1 vanilla bean or 2 teaspoons pure vanilla extract

6 cups whole milk

¾ cup honey

Generous pinch of kosher salt

2 cups bourbon

1. Using a sharp paring knife, halve the vanilla bean lengthwise, scrape out the seeds, and put the bean halves and seeds in a 4- to 6-quart slow cooker. Add the milk, honey, and salt and cook for 2 hours on LOW.

2. Uncover the cooker and reduce the heat to WARM. Remove the vanilla bean halves and discard. Pour in the bourbon and serve from the slow cooker, still set on WARM.

Holds well on warm	Prep time: 10 minutes	Slow-cook time: 2 hours
	Finish time: 5 minutes	Equipment: 4- to 6-quart slow cooker

See the photo on page 45.

Mulled Pear and Apple Cider

Toasting the spices in a dry skillet before adding them to the cider intensifies their flavors. Black peppercorns add an unexpected but subtle spiciness.

3 cinnamon sticks

2 teaspoons cardamom pods

1 teaspoon coriander seeds

1 teaspoon whole allspice

½ teaspoon black peppercorns

½ teaspoon whole cloves

5 cups apple cider

3 cups pear juice or nectar

One 2-inch ginger knob, peeled

1 teaspoon pure vanilla extract

Pinch of kosher salt

1. In a small skillet over medium heat, toast the cinnamon sticks, cardamom pods, coriander, allspice, peppercorns, and cloves, stirring them and watching carefully so they don't burn, until very fragrant, about 3 minutes. Put the toasted spices on a piece of cheesecloth and tie them into a bundle using a piece of kitchen twine or a thin strip of cheesecloth. (If you don't have cheesecloth, it's not the end of the world; just put the spices directly in the cooker. But it's nicer to drink the cider without worrying about crunching on whole spices.)

2. Put the spice bundle into a 4- to 6-quart slow cooker. Add the cider, pear juice, ginger, vanilla, and salt, then cover and cook on HIGH for 2 hours. Reduce the heat to WARM, remove and discard the ginger knob with tongs or a slotted spoon (you can leave the spice bundle in there to infuse further, or remove and discard it if you prefer), and serve the cider from the slow cooker, still set on WARM.

Holds well on warm	Prep time: 10 minutes	Slow-cook time: 2 hours
	Finish time: 5 minutes	Equipment: 4- to 6-quart slow cooker and cheesecloth

Brown Buttered Rum

Traditional buttered rum is usually a warm mixture of rum, a little sugar, and melted butter. The only problem is that butter and rum don't emulsify, and the fat floats to the surface, which is not very appetizing, no matter how much you love butter. So some very smart bartenders like Eben Freeman came up with a technique called fat washing: You just combine a fat (any fat, even bacon drippings) with alcohol, let them sit together long enough for the fat's flavor to infuse into the alcohol, and then remove the solidified fat. This is a slow-cooker adaptation of Freeman's recipe for brown buttered rum: You let brown butter infuse into rum for 2 days and then use the infused rum to make a warm cocktail. It tastes like the essence of butterscotch.

4 cups dark spiced rum

1 pound (4 sticks) unsalted butter

¾ cup packed light brown sugar

2 generous pinches of kosher salt

1 vanilla bean

1. Pour the rum into a large jar or other heatproof, sealable container with a capacity of at least 7 cups. Melt the butter in a large skillet over medium-high heat. After the butter melts, continue to cook it, swirling the pan occasionally, until the foamy white butter solids start to turn golden brown and smell nutty. Some of the solids will sink to the bottom of the skillet, where they could start to burn, so watch carefully and turn off the heat as soon as the solids turn toasty and brown. Let the butter cool for a few seconds, then pour it into the rum and stir. Let the mixture cool completely at room temperature, then cover and refrigerate for 2 days.

2. Line a fine-mesh strainer with cheesecloth. Using a large spoon, poke a hole in the solidified butter on top of the rum and strain the rum directly into a 4- to 6-quart slow cooker. (If you don't have cheesecloth, strain it twice through the strainer.)

3. Add 5 cups water to the slow cooker. Stir in the sugar and salt. Using a sharp paring knife, halve the vanilla bean lengthwise, scrape out the seeds, and add the bean halves and seeds to the slow cooker. Cover and cook on LOW for 1 hour, until just warmed through (don't let it come close to a simmer). Reduce the heat to WARM, uncover, remove and discard the vanilla bean halves with a slotted spoon, and serve.

Holds well on warm	Prep time: 20 minutes plus 2 days infusing	Slow-cook time: 1 hour	Equipment: 4- to 6-quart slow cooker and cheesecloth

LEFT: Granola with Pistachios, Coconut, and Cardamom
RIGHT: Savory Granola with with Buckwheat, Cashews, and Curry

Breakfast and Brunch

I always thought I wasn't a morning person. Then I had a baby. Now I am a morning person, in the sense that I am very well acquainted with the morning. But being minimally conscious at 5 A.M. has not turned me into a breakfast maker. My husband is game to whip up pancakes or breakfast sandwiches. I'm more into shoveling last night's spaghetti into my face or piling an unwise amount of granola into a bowl of yogurt. That's one reason I love slow-cooker breakfasts: You don't have to make them in the morning. Steel-cut oatmeal or a strata can be ready the minute you wake up. And I love the delicate, creamy texture that custards (eggs plus milk) acquire when steamed in the slow cooker. Some of these recipes can cook all night and be ready in the morning, and they're marked so you can easily find them when that's what you need. Others, like the granolas, are best made on the weekend, so you can eat them all week. Still others cook for a few hours and are perfect for having people over for brunch.

All-night recipes: These recipes can cook or hold on warm unattended for 8 hours or more.

Granola with Pistachios, Coconut, and Cardamom

MAKES ABOUT 7 CUPS

Pregnancy gave me a wicked sweet tooth that has stuck around. During maternity leave, I became extremely attached to a sugary packaged pistachio and apricot granola. There were many problems with my eating 4 servings of granola for breakfast, including the fact that a bag cost over five dollars and I could go through it in 2 days. So I started making my own. It requires a little bit of stirring so all the ingredients toast evenly in the slow cooker, but it's something you can have going on in the background while you're doing other things and hardly even realize you're being productive and making breakfast for the week (or, you know, 2 days). Note that this is a loose granola, not a clustery granola.

½ cup coconut oil, plus extra for greasing

4 cups old-fashioned rolled oats

1 cup shelled unsalted pistachios

1 cup unsweetened coconut flakes (chips)

¾ cup pure maple syrup, the darker the better

1 teaspoon ground cardamom

1 teaspoon ground cinnamon

1 teaspoon ground nutmeg

1 teaspoon kosher salt

1 cup sliced dried apricots (about 5 ounces)

1. Generously grease a 5- to 8-quart slow cooker with the oil. Add the oats, pistachios, and coconut flakes and toss to evenly combine.

2. In a small saucepan over medium heat, melt the ½ cup oil. Stir in the maple syrup, cardamom, cinnamon, nutmeg, and salt. Add the spiced coconut oil to the slow cooker and toss to evenly coat the oat mixture. Set the slow cooker lid ajar, leaving a gap of about 2 inches. (The vent prevents the granola from getting soggy.) Cook the granola on HIGH until well toasted, about 2 hours, stirring every 30 minutes so that it doesn't burn around the edges.

3. Pour the granola out onto a baking sheet. Toss in the apricots and spread out the mixture evenly. Cool the granola completely to room temperature, then store it in an airtight container at room temperature for up to 2 weeks.

Good to know: Feel free to use the same quantity of a different nut or a different dried fruit, if you prefer.

Does not hold well on warm	Prep time: 10 minutes	Slow-cook time: 2 hours, with occasional stirring
	Finish time: 5 minutes plus cooling	Equipment: 5- to 8-quart slow cooker

See the photo on page 54.

Savory Granola with Buckwheat, Cashews, and Curry

MAKES ABOUT 7 CUPS

Sprinkle this spiced granola on yogurt for breakfast or use it anytime as a crunchy topping for salads or dal, like the one on page 108. Like the sweet version on the previous page, this makes a loose, crunchy cereal, not one with clusters.

2½ cups old-fashioned rolled oats

1½ cups unsalted cashews

1 cup raw, hulled pumpkin seeds (pepitas)

½ cup whole raw, hulled buckwheat groats

2½ teaspoons curry powder

2 teaspoons fennel seeds

1 teaspoon red pepper flakes

Kosher salt

½ cup olive or canola oil

2 tablespoons honey

1 cup raisins

1. Combine the oats, cashews, pumpkin seeds, buckwheat groats, curry powder, fennel seeds, red pepper flakes, and 1¾ teaspoons salt in a 5- to 8-quart slow cooker and stir to combine evenly.

2. In a medium bowl or liquid measuring cup, whisk together the oil and honey. Pour it over the dry ingredients in the slow cooker and then mix to evenly moisten all of the granola. Set the lid ajar by about 2 inches (the vent will prevent sogginess) and cook on **HIGH** until well toasted, about 2 hours, stirring every 30 minutes to make sure the granola doesn't burn around the edges.

3. Pour the granola out onto a baking sheet. Toss in the raisins and spread out the mixture evenly. Cool the granola to room temperature, then store it in an airtight container at room temperature for up to 2 weeks.

Does not hold well on warm	Prep time: 10 minutes	Slow-cook time: 2 hours, with occasional stirring
	Finish time: 5 minutes plus cooling	Equipment: 5- to 8-quart slow cooker

See the photo on page 54.

Egg, Cheese, and Everything Bagel Strata (aka NYC Bodega Special)

This is a breakfast casserole version of the ubiquitous egg-and-cheese you can get at every bodega, coffee cart, and bagel shop here in New York. The American cheese makes it authentic, so don't try to fancy it up, please! I've provided a range of times and temperatures so that you can let it go overnight if you want to wake up to a ready-to-go breakfast or have it ready in 2 hours 30 minutes (on high) or 4 hours (on low). I feel that the 4 hours on low is the best option when possible, but surprisingly, all three options work very well. Don't skip the foil collar; it prevents the edges from getting too dark.

3 large everything bagels (12 to 13 ounces total), cut into 1-inch pieces

8 ounces American cheese, chopped small (about 2 heaping cups)

4 ounces sharp cheddar cheese, grated (about 1 heaping cup)

10 large eggs

2 cups whole milk

1¾ teaspoons kosher salt

Freshly ground black pepper

1. Preheat the oven to 300°F. Spread out the bagel pieces on a rimmed baking sheet and bake until quite dry, 15 to 20 minutes.

2. Meanwhile, prepare a 5- to 7-quart slow cooker: Fold a large piece of foil into a 3 × 12-inch strip and press it against the side of the insert that runs the hottest, using the foil like a collar or a shield. The hot spot is probably the wall of the insert opposite (farthest from) the control panel. This will keep that side of the strata from scorching or cooking too quickly. If your slow cooker runs very hot and tends to overbrown on all sides, line the other side with a foil collar as well (see page xxv for a how-to). Then line the entire insert with 1 piece of parchment, making sure the parchment comes up at least 2 inches on all sides (see page xxvi for a how-to). This is to prevent sticking and also to make it easier to reach in and remove the strata. (You're using 1 piece of parchment so that the egg mixture doesn't run between 2 layers of parchment when you pour it in.)

3. Put half the bagel pieces into the prepared insert. Top with half the cheeses. Put the remaining bagel pieces on top and then the remaining cheeses. In a medium bowl or large liquid measuring cup, beat together the eggs and milk. Season with the salt and several generous grinds of pepper. Pour the egg mixture over the bagels and cheese, keeping all the

liquid contained in the parchment liner and making sure all the bagel pieces are moistened. Cover and cook until the custard is just set but still jiggly in the middle: on **HIGH** for 2 hours followed by **WARM** for 6 hours; on **HIGH** for 2 hours 30 minutes; or on **LOW** for 4 hours.

4. Uncover the slow cooker and turn it off. Let the strata rest for about 10 minutes. Grabbing the edges of the parchment liner, lift the strata out of the insert and put it on a cutting board. Serve warm or at room temperature, cut into wedges.

ALL-NIGHT	Holds well on warm through step 3 for up to 30 additional minutes	Prep time: 20 minutes	Slow-cook time: 8 hours, 4 hours, or 2 hours 30 minutes (see timing notes in recipe instructions)	Equipment: 5- to 7-quart slow cooker

Grainy Bread Strata with Kale and Gruyère

This satisfying breakfast casserole walks a line between wholesome (kale, whole grain bread) and indulgent (a lot of cheese). Gruyère (Queen of Cheeses!) melts beautifully and has a nutty, complex flavor. It can be expensive, though, so you could substitute more-affordable fontina or use a mix of the two. I've given a range of times and heat levels so that you can make the strata work with your breakfast schedule.

10 ounces crusty, rustic multigrain bread (about ½ rustic loaf or 3 large rolls), cut into 1- to 2-inch cubes (6 to 7 cups)

1 bunch of kale (8 to 10 ounces), stemmed

10 large eggs, beaten

2 cups whole milk

1 teaspoon red pepper flakes

2 teaspoons kosher salt

Freshly ground black pepper

12 ounces Gruyère, grated (about 3 heaping cups)

1. Preheat the oven to 300°F. Spread the bread pieces on a rimmed baking sheet and toast in the oven for about 30 minutes, until very dry.

2. Meanwhile, prepare a 5- to 7-quart slow cooker: Fold a large piece of foil into a 3 × 12-inch strip and press it against the side of the insert that runs the hottest, using the foil like a collar or a shield. The hot spot is probably the wall of the insert opposite (farthest from) the control panel. This will keep that side of the strata from scorching or cooking too quickly. If your slow cooker runs very hot and tends to overbrown on all sides, line the other side with a foil collar as well (see page xxv for a how-to). Then line the entire insert with 1 piece of parchment, making sure the parchment comes up at least 2 inches on all sides (see page xxvi for a how-to). This is to prevent sticking and also to make it easier to reach in and remove the strata. (You're using 1 piece of parchment so that the egg mixture doesn't run between 2 layers of parchment when you pour it in.)

3. Bring a large pot of salted water to a boil. Add the kale leaves, give them a stir, cover, and cook until just wilted, about 1 minute. Drain the kale in a colander, run under cold water to stop the cooking, and thoroughly squeeze the water out with your hands; then blot the kale dry with a kitchen or paper towel. Chop the kale and set it aside.

4. In a medium bowl or large liquid measuring cup, beat together the eggs and milk. Add the red pepper flakes, salt, and a few generous grinds of pepper.

5. Put half the bread pieces into the bottom of the prepared insert. Scatter all the kale and half of the cheese over the top. Add the remaining bread and top with the remaining cheese. Carefully pour the egg mixture all over the top, keeping all the liquid contained in the parchment liner and making sure all the pieces of bread are moistened. Cook until the custard is just set but still jiggly in the middle: on HIGH for 2 hours followed by WARM for 6 hours; on HIGH for 2 hours 30 minutes; or on LOW for 4 hours.

6. Uncover the slow cooker and turn it off. Let the strata rest for 10 minutes. Grabbing the edges of the parchment liner, lift the strata out of the insert. Serve warm or at room temperature, cut into wedges.

| ALL-NIGHT | Holds well on warm through step 5 for up to 30 additional minutes | Prep time: 20 minutes | Slow-cook time: 8 hours, 4 hours, or 2 hours 30 minutes (see timing notes in recipe instructions) |
| | | Finish time: 5 minutes | Equipment: 5- to 7-quart slow cooker |

Apple Spice Overnight Oatmeal with Hazelnuts

MAKES ABOUT 5 CUPS

Steel-cut oats get tender and creamy when cooked overnight. Set your cooker for low heat for 2 hours and then let it auto-switch to warm and cook gently for the rest of the night. (You can also just cook the oats on low for 4 hours if you don't need the overnight timing.) You can make the apple mix-in the night before and let it sit at room temperature all night, or you can do it right before serving.

4 tablespoons (½ stick) unsalted butter, plus more for greasing

1 cup uncooked steel-cut oats

½ cup unsweetened applesauce

2 teaspoons ground cardamom

1 teaspoon ground cinnamon

¼ teaspoon ground cloves

Kosher salt

1 pound apples (2 to 3 large), peeled, cored, and thinly sliced (see note, below)

1 cup coarsely chopped unsalted hazelnuts

1 teaspoon finely grated nutmeg

½ teaspoon ground allspice

⅓ cup pure maple syrup, the darker the better, plus more to taste and for serving

Juice of ¼ lemon

1. Generously butter a 5- to 7-quart slow cooker. Add the oats and 4 cups water. Stir in the applesauce, 1 teaspoon of the cardamom, the cinnamon, cloves, and ¾ teaspoon salt. Cover and cook until the oatmeal is thick and tender: on LOW for about 4 hours or on LOW for 2 hours followed by WARM for 6 to 7 hours.

2. In a large skillet, melt the 4 tablespoons butter over medium-high heat. Add the apples and cook, stirring occasionally, until softened, about 8 minutes. Add the hazelnuts and cook, stirring, until toasted, 3 minutes. Add the nutmeg, the remaining 1 teaspoon cardamom, the allspice, and ½ teaspoon salt. Reduce the heat to low and cook, stirring, about 1 minute, until fragrant. You can do this just before serving or the day before, in which case store the apple mixture in an airtight container at room temperature.

3. Stir the apple mixture into the cooked oatmeal. Add the maple syrup and lemon juice. Taste and add more salt or maple syrup if you like. Serve with additional maple syrup at the table.

Good to know: Any kind of apple will work in this recipe, but I prefer crisp, sweet-tart apples that hold their shape when cooked, like Honeycrisp or Granny Smith. Softer apples like McIntosh tend to disintegrate.

| ALL-NIGHT | Holds well on warm through step 1 for up to 1 additional hour | Prep time: 10 minutes | Slow-cook time: 4 hours or 9 hours |
| | | Finish time: 20 minutes | Equipment: 5- to 7-quart slow cooker |

TOP: Apple Spice Overnight
Oatmeal with Hazelnuts
BOTTOM: Savory Oatmeal with
Bacon, Scallions, and Cheddar, 66

Savory Oatmeal with Bacon, Scallions, and Cheddar

MAKES ABOUT 5 CUPS

This savory oatmeal is reminiscent of cheesy grits: very creamy and rich with little bits of crisp bacon. An egg on top is terrific if you like your lilies gilded.

Butter, for greasing

1 cup uncooked steel-cut oats

Kosher salt

½ pound thick-cut bacon

5 scallions, trimmed, light green and white parts thinly sliced, plus the dark green parts, sliced for topping

8 ounces sharp cheddar, grated (about 2 heaping cups)

Freshly ground black pepper

Fried or poached eggs, for topping (1 per person; optional)

1. Generously butter a 5- to 7-quart slow cooker. Add the oats, 4 cups water, and ¾ teaspoon salt. Cook until the oatmeal is thick and tender: on LOW for 4 hours or on LOW for 2 hours followed by WARM for 6 to 7 hours.

2. Put the bacon into a cold large skillet and bring the heat to medium. Cook, flipping a couple times, until the bacon has rendered a lot of its fat and is deeply browned and crisp, about 10 minutes. Drain on paper towels, then coarsely chop. You can do this right before serving the oatmeal or the day before, in which case store the crisped bacon in an airtight container in the refrigerator and bring it to room temperature before using.

3. When the oatmeal is done, stir in the bacon, white and light green scallion slices, and about three-quarters of the cheese (about 6 ounces). Taste for seasoning and add more salt if necessary and a few grinds of pepper. Serve in bowls topped with the remaining cheese, the dark green sliced scallions, and eggs, if you like.

ALL-NIGHT	Holds well on warm through step 1 for up to 1 additional hour	Prep time: 5 minutes	Slow-cook time: 4 hours or 9 hours
		Finish time: 20 minutes	Equipment: 5- to 7-quart slow cooker

See the photo on page 65.

Crustless Quiche with Smoked Salmon, Goat Cheese, and Scallions

MAKES 6 TO 8 SERVINGS

This simple crustless quiche is not the most beautiful thing in the world, but it makes up for its looks in spectacular texture: The slow steam makes it delicate and custardy. It's good warm, at room temperature, or cold, so you could make it for a brunch and leave it out on a buffet without worrying much about timing.

9 large eggs

½ cup crème fraîche or sour cream

1¼ cups whole milk

Kosher salt

3 scallions, white and light green parts only, trimmed and thinly sliced

4 ounces sliced cold-smoked salmon, chopped (heaping ½ cup)

3 ounces fresh goat cheese (about ¾ cup crumbled)

1. Prepare a 5- to 6-quart slow cooker: Fold a large piece of foil into a 3 × 12-inch strip and press it against the side of the insert that runs the hottest, using the foil like a collar or a shield. The hot spot is probably the wall of the insert opposite (farthest from) the control panel. This will keep that side of the quiche from scorching or cooking too quickly. If your slow cooker runs very hot and tends to overbrown on all sides, line the other side with a foil collar as well (see page xxv for a how-to). Then line the entire insert with 1 piece of parchment, making sure the parchment comes up at least 2 inches on all sides (see page xxvi for a how-to). This is to prevent sticking and also to make it easier to reach in and remove the quiche. (You're using 1 piece of parchment so that the egg mixture doesn't run between 2 layers of parchment when you pour it in.)

2. In a large bowl, whisk together the eggs and crème fraîche until smooth. Whisk in the milk and 1½ teaspoons salt. Stir in the scallions and salmon and pour into the prepared slow cooker, keeping all the liquid contained in the parchment liner. Crumble the goat cheese evenly over the custard. Cover and cook until the custard is just set but still jiggly in the middle: on **HIGH** for 2 hours to 2 hours 30 minutes or on **LOW** for about 3 hours 30 minutes.

3. Uncover the slow cooker and turn it off. Let the quiche cool for a few minutes. Grabbing the edges of the parchment liner, carefully lift the quiche out of the insert. Serve warm, at room temperature, or cold, cut into slices.

Holds well on warm through step 2 for up to 30 minutes	Prep time: 10 minutes	Slow-cook time: 2 hours to 3 hours 30 minutes	Equipment: 5- to 6-quart slow cooker

Spanish Tortilla Sandwiches with Manchego and Red Pepper Aioli

MAKES 6 SERVINGS

This is my simplified version of a Spanish tortilla, which is like a potato and onion frittata. It's an extremely handy thing to have around, because it's good cold, at room temperature, or warm and keeps for up to 4 days in the fridge. I like it very much as a breakfast or brunch sandwich on ciabatta with this quick red pepper aioli, but that's too carb-on-carb for some people. If that's you, just skip the bread and eat the tortilla drizzled with the aioli.

TORTILLA

¼ cup extra-virgin olive oil

1 large yellow onion, halved and thinly sliced

Kosher salt

4 medium Yukon Gold potatoes (about 1½ pounds), unpeeled and thinly sliced

2 garlic cloves, finely chopped

Freshly ground black pepper

10 large eggs

4 ounces manchego cheese, grated (1 heaping cup)

AIOLI AND SANDWICHES

2 tablespoons drained, diced jarred roasted red peppers

½ garlic clove, grated or minced

½ cup mayonnaise

Ciabatta rolls (1 per serving)

1. Prepare a 5- to 7-quart slow cooker: Fold a large piece of foil into a 3 × 12-inch strip and press it against the side of the insert that runs the hottest, using the foil like a collar or a shield. The hot spot is probably the wall of the insert opposite (farthest from) the control panel. This will keep that side of the tortilla from scorching or cooking too quickly. If your slow cooker runs very hot and tends to overbrown on all sides, line the other side with a foil collar as well (see page xxv for a how-to). Then line the entire insert with 1 piece of parchment, making sure the parchment comes up at least 2 inches on all sides (see page xxvi for a how-to). This is to prevent sticking and also to make it easier to reach in and remove the tortilla. (You're using 1 piece of parchment so that the egg mixture doesn't run between 2 layers of parchment when you pour it in.)

2. To make the tortilla, in a large skillet, warm the oil over medium-high heat. Add the onion, season generously with salt, and cook, stirring, until quite soft and translucent, about 10 minutes. Add the potatoes and garlic and stir well to combine so that the potato slices aren't sticking together too much. Season lightly with salt and very generously with black pepper. Reduce the heat to medium, cover the pan, and cook, stirring once or twice, until the potatoes are just starting to approach tender but are still underdone, about 10 minutes. Scrape the potato-onion mixture into the prepared slow cooker and spread it out evenly.

3. Beat the eggs with ½ teaspoon salt and season them very generously with pepper. Pour the eggs over the onion mixture, keeping all the liquid contained in the parchment liner. Cover and cook on LOW until just

fully set, about 2 hours 30 minutes to 3 hours. (You can also cook this on HIGH for about 1 hour 30 minutes to 2 hours, but it cooks more evenly on low heat.)

4. Sprinkle the cheese over the top of the tortilla. Cover the slow cooker and let the cheese just soften on WARM heat, about 2 minutes. (You don't want it to fully melt because it'll break, which isn't the end of the world but will result in little pools of oil on top of the tortilla, which you'll then want to blot off.) Uncover the slow cooker and turn it off. Let the tortilla cool for a few minutes. Grabbing the edges of the parchment liner, lift the tortilla out of the insert.

5. To make the aioli, puree the roasted red peppers, garlic, and mayonnaise using either a mini–food processor or an immersion blender set in a measuring cup. (You can also just mince the peppers and garlic and then stir them into the mayo in a small bowl.)

6. Serve the tortilla warm or at room temperature. For sandwiches, spread sliced ciabatta rolls with the aioli and tuck slices of the tortilla inside. (Or simply serve wedges of the tortilla drizzled with the aioli.) To store leftovers, let the tortilla cool to room temperature, then wrap in plastic and store in the refrigerator for up to 4 days.

| Holds on warm through step 3 for up to 2 hours | Prep time: 30 minutes | Slow-cook time: 2 hours or 3 hours |
| | Finish time: 10 minutes | Equipment: 5- to 7-quart slow cooker |

Pumpkin Challah French Toast Bake

This is basically a pumpkin pie breakfast bread pudding. It will not look pretty coming out of the slow cooker—don't worry, a dusting of confectioners' sugar and a sprinkling of pecans does wonders.

1 challah loaf (10 to 12 ounces), cut into 1- to 2-inch chunks (about 9 cups)

6 large eggs

One 15-ounce can pure pumpkin puree (not pumpkin pie mix)

½ cup granulated sugar

1 cup half-and-half

1 tablespoon pure vanilla extract

1 teaspoon ground cinnamon

½ teaspoon ground allspice

½ teaspoon finely grated nutmeg

Kosher salt

Confectioners' sugar, for topping

1 cup pecans, toasted (recipe follows) and chopped, for topping

Pure maple syrup, for serving

1. Preheat the oven to 300°F. Spread the bread pieces on a rimmed baking sheet and bake until they are very dry and crisp, about 30 minutes.

2. Meanwhile, prepare a 5- to 7-quart slow cooker: Fold a large piece of foil into a 3 × 12-inch strip and press it against the side of the insert that runs the hottest, using the foil like a collar or a shield. The hot spot is probably the wall of the insert opposite (farthest from) the control panel. This will keep that side of the French toast from scorching or cooking too quickly. If your slow cooker runs very hot and tends to overbrown on all sides, line the other side with a foil collar as well (see page xxv for a how-to). Then line the entire insert with 1 piece of parchment, making sure the parchment comes up at least 2 inches on all sides (see page xxvi for a how-to). This is to prevent sticking and also to make it easier to reach in and remove the French toast. (You're using 1 piece of parchment so that the egg mixture doesn't run between 2 layers of parchment when you pour it in.)

3. Whisk together the eggs, pumpkin, granulated sugar, half-and-half, vanilla, cinnamon, allspice, nutmeg, and ½ teaspoon salt. Put the bread into the prepared cooker. Pour the egg mixture all over the bread, keeping all the liquid contained in the parchment liner and making sure all the bread gets moistened, pressing the bread down into the liquid if necessary. Cover and cook until the custard is just set: on HIGH for 2 hours 30 minutes, on LOW for 4 hours, or on HIGH for 1 hour 30 minutes followed by WARM for 7 hours.

4. Uncover and turn off the slow cooker. Let the French toast cool for a few minutes. Grabbing the edges of the parchment liner, lift the French toast out of the insert and place it on a serving platter. Dust it with confectioners' sugar and top it with the pecans. Serve with maple syrup.

TOASTED NUTS

Scatter nuts into a large dry skillet over medium heat and toast, stirring often, until the nuts darken slightly in spots and smell toasty, about 3 minutes. Don't walk away! The nuts will burn quickly.

ALL-NIGHT	Holds on warm through step 3 for up to 1 hour	Prep time: 35 minutes	Slow-cook time: 2 hours 30 minutes, 4 hours, or 8 hours 30 minutes
		Finish time: 5 minutes	Equipment: 5- to 7-quart slow cooker

Chorizo Cassoulet with
Spicy Bread Crumbs

Weeknight Dinners

Weeknight dinners are the heart of slow cooking. Throw something in the pot at the beginning of the day, go to work, and come home to a hot meal. No matter how much you love to cook, even if you're one of those people who starts fantasizing about lunch right after breakfast, there are nights when dinner is a problem to be solved rather than a pleasure. That's true of everyone, even people who have dedicated their whole lives to cooking. You don't have to give up your food-lover card if there are some nights when you can't quite figure out what's for dinner.

This is the chapter that solves that problem, at least partially. I have spent a lot of time with slow cookers now. (There are six in my small Brooklyn apartment and I'm pretty sure our babysitters think I'm insane. I'm writing a cookbook, I swear!) I have good news and bad news. The good news is that if you have about fifteen minutes in the morning and fifteen minutes at night, there are plenty of recipes in this chapter that can cook unattended for about eight hours in between. The bad news is that there are very few cases in which you can put a bunch of raw ingredients into the cooker and then come home and eat them without doing anything else to them—at least not without a substantial compromise in taste or texture. You may need to sauté the aromatics in the morning before putting everything in the pot to make dal, for instance. Or run chicken under the broiler to crisp the skin at night. Often, these upgrades take a matter of minutes and make a huge difference in the final dish.

I've also taken into account the fact that not everyone works in an office from nine to five. The gig economy has changed work schedules for a lot of people, myself included, so you'll find some recipes that cook for three, four, or five hours in here. Some of them can hold on warm, making them good choices for people who are away all day, and some of them can't. The ones that can cook for eight hours or more are marked "All-Day" so you can find them easily if that's what you need.

Pick and choose what works best for your family and your schedule, and keep in mind that these recipes are also jumping-off points—once you know that the slow cooker can make a wonderfully fragrant infused oil for poaching fish, you really don't need me to tell you how to flavor the oil and which fish to use. Once you know you can steam a big batch of farro in the slow cooker and then keep it on hand for no-cook grain bowls, you can decide for yourself that you'd prefer a handful of arugula with it rather than the marinated kale I've suggested. I hope these recipes will make the daily practice of feeding yourself and your loved ones more of a pleasure.

*All-day recipes: These recipes can cook or hold on warm
unattended for 8 hours or more.*

Grains, Beans, and Pasta

Roasted Red Pepper, Caper, Walnut, and Tahini Grain Bowl, 82

Summer Tomato, Basil, and Burrata Grain Bowl, 81

Marinated Kale, Pecorino, and Smoked Almond Grain Bowl, 81

Smoked Salmon and Everything Bagel Spice Grain Bowl, 80

Avocado and Grapefruit Grain Bowl with Coconut-Lime Vinaigrette, 82

No-Cook Grain Bowls

Grain bowls are practical, healthy, and customizable—having a stash of steamed grains in the fridge means you are never far from a good meal. You'll find directions for steaming various whole grains in the slow cooker in the Basics and Building Blocks chapter (page 1). These bowls are ideal for no-cook suppers or portable lunches—each works with whatever grain you have on hand or like best. I like to use room-temperature grains, but you could also use just-cooked or chilled grains. Plan to use one cup, more or less, of grain per bowl; there's no need to measure. Just pile grains in a bowl according to your appetite and then top it following one of the ideas below.

Smoked Salmon and Everything Bagel Spice Grain Bowl

TO MAKE 1 BOWL: Pile the steamed **grains** of your choice in a bowl. (Barley or farro is great here.) Add a small handful of **baby arugula** and about 2 ounces sliced **smoked salmon**. Drizzle some **Lemon Yogurt Dressing** (recipe follows) over everything, then top with a sprinkle of **everything bagel spice**.

LEMON YOGURT DRESSING   MAKES 4 SERVINGS

In a medium bowl, whisk ½ cup plain whole milk or 2% **Greek yogurt**, ½ small grated **garlic clove**, 2 tablespoons **lemon juice** (from about ½ lemon), 1 tablespoon **water**, 1 tablespoon **olive oil**, and ½ teaspoon **kosher salt** (or to taste). Whisk in more water or lemon juice to thin the dressing if necessary.

See the photo on page 79.

Summer Tomato, Basil, and Burrata Grain Bowl

TO MAKE 1 BOWL: Pile the steamed **grains** of your choice in a bowl. (Barley or farro is great here.) Add ½ chopped **ripe tomato**, a handful of torn **basil**, one-quarter of an 8-ounce **burrata** ball, the juice of ½ **lemon**, and a good glug of **olive oil**. Season with **salt** and **pepper**. Stir so that the cream from the *burrata* sauces the whole bowl.

See the photo on page 78.

Marinated Kale, Pecorino, and Smoked Almond Grain Bowl

TO MAKE 1 BOWL: Pile the steamed **grains** of your choice in a bowl. (Spelt or farro is great here.) Drizzle the grains with **olive oil**, then top with a generous shower of grated **pecorino Romano**. Top with a handful of **Marinated Kale** (recipe follows), then more grated pecorino. Finish with a small handful of chopped **smoked almonds**.

MARINATED KALE   MAKES 4 SERVINGS

Wash, dry, and stem 1 large bunch of **kale** (I prefer lacinato), then cut the leaves into thin ribbons and put the ribbons into a sealable container or zip-top bag. Add the juice of 1 large **lemon**, 3 tablespoons **olive oil**, 1 teaspoon **kosher salt**, and 1 teaspoon **red pepper flakes**. Massage all the ingredients together, then close the container or seal the bag and shake. Let sit for at least 30 minutes or refrigerate for up to 1 day before serving.

See the photo on page 79.

Avocado and Grapefruit Grain Bowl with Coconut-Lime Vinaigrette

TO MAKE 1 BOWL: Pile the steamed **grains** of your choice in a bowl. (Black rice is great here.) Add the segments from ½ **grapefruit** (peel, pith, and membrane cut away) and one-quarter of a sliced **avocado**. Season with **salt**. Drizzle with **Coconut-Lime Vinaigrette** (recipe follows). Top with salted **cashews**.

COCONUT-LIME VINAIGRETTE   MAKES 4 SERVINGS

Whisk together ¼ cup fresh **lime juice** (from about 2 limes) and ½ cup plus 1 tablespoon well-shaken full-fat **coconut milk**. Add 1 tablespoon plain whole milk **Greek yogurt** and ½ teaspoon **kosher salt**. Whisk to combine and stir in 1 seeded, diced **jalapeño**. Add a bit more yogurt if you'd like a thicker dressing.

See the photo on page 79.

Roasted Red Pepper, Caper, Walnut, and Tahini Grain Bowl

TO MAKE 1 BOWL: Pile the steamed **grains** of your choice in a bowl. (Brown rice is great here.) Add ⅓ cup chopped **roasted red peppers** and 1½ teaspoons **capers**. Top with 1 tablespoon **tahini** and the juice of ½ **lemon** and season with **salt** and **pepper**. Toss well until everything is evenly combined and creamy. Top with 2 tablespoons chopped **toasted walnuts** (see page 72 for toasting directions) and some chopped fresh **parsley** and/or **dill**.

See the photo on page 78.

Chorizo Cassoulet with Spicy Bread Crumbs

MAKES 4 SERVINGS

This wintry ragout isn't a traditional cassoulet, but it's reminiscent of all the things I love about the classic dish: the creamy flageolet beans enriched with pork, the crunchy bread-crumb topping. It's an ideal, comforting cold-weather weeknight dinner—wholesome but not at all austere. Old beans can dry out to the point where they will not become tender no matter how long you cook them, so it's worth buying a new bag if yours has been hanging around for a long time.

1¾ cups dried flageolet beans (about 12 ounces)

5 garlic cloves, smashed

1½ teaspoons smoked paprika

½ teaspoon ground cumin

Kosher salt and freshly ground black pepper

3¾ cups Classic Chicken Stock (page 5), low-sodium chicken broth, or water

6 ounces dried Spanish chorizo sausage, diced small

1 bunch of kale (8 to 10 ounces), preferably lacinato, stemmed and roughly chopped

1 tablespoon unsalted butter

1 teaspoon red pepper flakes, or to taste

1 cup panko bread crumbs, for topping

1. Cover the beans with water by at least 1 inch in a large saucepan and bring them to a boil. Lower the heat to medium-low and let them gently simmer for 10 minutes, then drain.

2. Combine the drained beans, garlic, 1 teaspoon of the paprika, the cumin, 1½ teaspoons salt (use only 1 teaspoon if you're using store-bought salted broth), and a few generous grinds of black pepper in a 5- to 8-quart slow cooker. Add the chicken stock and stir to combine. Cover and cook on LOW until the beans are tender but not falling apart, 8 to 9 hours. (Check them early if you can; there is a wide time range in which beans become tender. In general, larger slow cookers will cook faster than smaller ones.)

3. About 20 minutes before you eat, increase the heat to HIGH and stir in the chorizo and kale. Cook until the kale is tender, about 15 minutes.

4. Meanwhile, in a small skillet, melt the butter over medium-high heat. Add the remaining ½ teaspoon paprika and the red pepper flakes and stir to combine. Add the panko and cook, stirring, until the bread crumbs are orange from the spices and lightly toasted, about 1 minute. Season the spiced bread crumbs with salt.

5. Serve the cassoulet in bowls and top each portion with a generous sprinkle of the bread crumbs.

Good to know: If you can't find flageolet beans, you can substitute an equal amount of cannellini beans, but because they are larger they will take a bit longer to cook—allow 8 to 10 hours for them to get tender.

| ALL-DAY | Holds well on warm through step 2 or step 3 for up to 2 hours | Prep time: 15 minutes | Slow-cook time: 8 to 9 hours |
| | | Finish time: 20 minutes | Equipment: 5- to 8-quart slow cooker |

See the photo on page 74.

Lentil Salad with Smoked Trout and Avocado

Without the avocado, this salad keeps well for up to 4 days—just toss in the avocado right before you eat. It's equally good warm or at room temperature, so it makes an excellent packed lunch.

1½ cups beluga lentils (about 12 ounces)

Kosher salt and freshly ground black pepper

12 ounces jarred roasted red peppers, drained and chopped (about 1 heaping cup)

8 ounces smoked trout fillets, skinned and flaked

½ cup chopped fresh flat-leaf parsley

⅓ cup minced fresh chives

3 tablespoons olive oil

3 tablespoons sherry vinegar, plus more to taste

1 ripe avocado, halved, pitted, peeled, and diced

Juice of ½ lemon

1. Combine the lentils with 4 cups water and 2 teaspoons salt in a 5- to 7-quart slow cooker. Cover and cook on LOW until the lentils are just tender but still hold their shape, about 3 hours. Drain. You can make the salad now, or the lentils can be refrigerated in a sealed container for up to 4 days.

2. In a serving bowl, combine the drained lentils with all the remaining ingredients. (If you're making the salad ahead of time, hold back the avocado.) Toss gently to combine. Taste and season with salt, pepper, and additional vinegar if you think it needs it. Serve warm, at room temperature, or cold.

Good to know: Beluga lentils are worth seeking out. Sometimes they're just labeled "black lentils," but you'll know them by the way they look—like little beads of caviar. They're tiny, firm, and jet black, and they keep their shape much better than other lentils, making them excellent in salads. Whole Foods and Trader Joe's both carry them, as does Amazon.

Does not hold well on warm	Prep time: 5 minutes	Slow-cook time: 3 hours
	Finish time: 20 minutes	Equipment: 5- to 7-quart slow cooker

Creamy Barley with Corn and Green Chile-Lime Salsa

This risotto-like whole grain ragout showcases the bright flavors of late summer: corn, tomatoes, and peppers. You can make it with 4 cups of frozen corn when fresh is out of season, but you'll miss out on the flavor the cobs add to the broth as it cooks.

4 large, plump ears fresh corn

4 cups Classic Chicken Stock (page 5), low-sodium chicken or vegetable broth, or water

2 tablespoons unsalted butter

6 large garlic cloves, chopped

1 large red or yellow onion, diced

Kosher salt and freshly ground black pepper

2 poblano peppers, stemmed, seeded, and thinly sliced

1½ cups pearled barley

1 cup dry white wine

2 scallions, trimmed and thinly sliced

2 medium ripe beefsteak or heirloom tomatoes, chopped

½ cup Mexican crema or sour cream

⅓ cup chopped fresh cilantro

One 7-ounce can diced green chiles, drained

2 jalapeños, stemmed, seeded, and diced

Juice of 1 lime

1. Cut the kernels from the corn cobs (you'll end up with 3 to 4 cups, depending on the size of the ears) and reserve the kernels in the fridge. Put the corn cobs into a 5- to 8-quart slow cooker (snap them in half if you need to) and add the stock.

2. Melt the butter in a large skillet over medium-high heat. Add the garlic and onion, season generously with salt and pepper, and cook, stirring occasionally, until the onion is softened and starting to brown, about 8 minutes. Add the poblanos, season with salt, and cook, stirring occasionally, until starting to soften, about 2 minutes. Add the barley and cook, stirring, to mix all the ingredients and to lightly toast the barley, 1 minute. Pour in the wine and cook, stirring and scraping up any browned bits on the bottom of the pan, until the liquid starts to bubble, about 1 minute. Season with salt and pepper again, then add the mixture to the slow cooker and stir to combine.

3. Cook on HIGH until the barley is tender, 2 hours 30 minutes to 3 hours. (Don't try to use low heat; it does not work well for grains.)

4. Reduce the heat to WARM if the slow cooker hasn't auto-switched. Using tongs, remove the corn cobs and use a spoon to scrape any barley off them back into the pot. Discard the cobs. Stir in the corn kernels and scallions and cook until the corn is just tender, 5 to 10 minutes. Stir in the tomatoes, crema, and cilantro.

5. In a medium bowl, stir together the canned chiles, jalapeños, and lime juice. Season with salt. Serve the barley in bowls topped with the salsa.

Good to know: You can make this dish completely vegetarian by using water or vegetable stock.

| Holds well on warm through step 3 for up to 30 minutes | Prep time: 25 minutes | Slow-cook time: 2 hours 30 minutes to 3 hours |
| | Finish time: 20 minutes | Equipment: 5- to 8-quart slow cooker |

Toby's Pizza Pasta with Black Garlic and Pancetta

MAKES 6 SERVINGS

Toby's Public House is our neighborhood pizza restaurant—it's pubbish and comfortable, with a long wooden bar and a wood-burning oven that turns out wonderful crisp-chewy pizzas. We always get a particular pie that's topped with tomato sauce, mushrooms, pancetta, mozzarella, and sweet black garlic (see note, opposite). This is that pizza translated into a baked pasta—make the sauce in the slow cooker and then just toss it with pasta and broil for a crisp, bubbly top.

4 ounces pancetta, diced

2 tablespoons olive oil

1 tablespoon unsalted butter

1 pound cremini mushrooms, stemmed and sliced

Kosher salt and freshly ground black pepper

2 tablespoons tomato paste

1 tablespoon balsamic vinegar

One 28-ounce can crushed tomatoes

1 teaspoon dried oregano

1 teaspoon red pepper flakes

1 pound large pasta shells

Cloves from 2 black garlic heads, halved

8 ounces fresh mozzarella, sliced, or, in a real pinch, preshredded mozzarella

1. Put the pancetta into a large dry skillet over medium-high heat and cook, stirring occasionally, until the fat renders and the bits start to get golden, about 4 minutes. Remove the pancetta with a slotted spoon, leaving its fat behind, and place it on a paper towel to drain. Reserve the crisped pancetta in the fridge.

2. Add the oil and butter to the skillet over medium-high heat and let the butter melt. Add the mushrooms, season with salt and pepper, and cook, stirring occasionally, until the mushrooms soften, give off their moisture, shrink, and start to brown, 8 to 10 minutes. Stir in the tomato paste and vinegar and cook, stirring, 1 minute. Add the tomatoes. Pour ¼ cup water into the can, swish it around to get out any remaining tomato, and add the water to the skillet. Stir in the oregano and red pepper flakes. Scrape the sauce into a 5- to 8-quart slow cooker and cover. Cook on LOW until the sauce's flavors have mellowed and married, about 6 hours.

3. Preheat the broiler on high and position a rack 6 inches from the heat source (if that's how your broiler is configured). Cook the pasta in boiling salted water until al dente, about 10 minutes.

4. Meanwhile, ladle the warm sauce into a 9 × 13-inch baking dish and toss in the black garlic cloves. Drain the pasta and toss it with the sauce. Taste and season with salt if necessary. Top the pasta evenly with the mozzarella slices and scatter the reserved crisp pancetta bits on top. Broil until the mozzarella is melted and browned in spots, 3 to 4 minutes.

Good to know: Black garlic is just regular garlic that's been aged until it has lost its pungency and become sweetish and soft, almost like a dried fruit. It's available at Trader Joe's, some Whole Foods, and Amazon.

ALL-DAY	Holds well on warm through step 2 for up to 3 hours	Prep time: 20 minutes	Slow-cook time: 6 hours
		Finish time: 20 minutes	Equipment: 5- to 8-quart slow cooker and a 9 × 13-inch oven-safe baking dish

Farro Puttanesca

This is a take on spaghetti puttanesca, a zingy, spicy, almost-vegetarian pasta from southern Italy that gets its big flavor from anchovies, capers, olives, garlic, tomato, and chile. This is my long-cooked, whole grain version, a risotto-like spicy farro dish. It's hearty enough to be a main dish on its own, but you could also serve this with a simple piece of baked fish or chicken on top.

1½ cups farro

One 28-ounce can crushed tomatoes, preferably fire-roasted

2 tablespoons capers plus 1 tablespoon caper pickling liquid or white wine vinegar

¼ cup plus 2 tablespoons extra-virgin olive oil

2 teaspoons red pepper flakes

1 teaspoon dried oregano

4 anchovy fillets

2 garlic cloves

1 teaspoon fennel seeds

Kosher salt and freshly ground black pepper

¾ cup pitted kalamata olives, halved

Juice of 1 lemon

Grated Parmesan and chopped fresh flat-leaf parsley, for topping

1. Place the farro in a 5- to 8-quart slow cooker and add the tomatoes. Pour 2¾ cups water into the tomato can, swish it around to get out any remaining tomato, and add the water to the slow cooker. Stir in the capers and their liquid, 2 tablespoons oil, 1 teaspoon of the red pepper flakes, and the oregano. Use a mortar and pestle to pound the anchovies, garlic, ½ teaspoon of the fennel seeds, and 1½ teaspoons salt until a paste forms, then stir in the paste. (Alternatively, finely mince the anchovies and garlic and add them to the slow cooker along with the salt and fennel.) Cover and cook on **HIGH** until the farro is tender, about 3 hours. (Don't try to use low heat; it does not work well for grains.)

2. Just before serving, pour the remaining ¼ cup oil into a small skillet over medium-high heat. Add the olives and cook, stirring, about 1 minute. (The olives will splutter.) Add the remaining 1 teaspoon red pepper flakes and remaining ½ teaspoon fennel seeds and cook, stirring, until fragrant, about 30 seconds. Stir the spiced olive oil mixture into the farro. Squeeze in the lemon juice. Serve in bowls topped with a sprinkling of Parmesan and parsley.

Holds well on warm through step 1 for up to 30 minutes	Prep time: 15 minutes	Slow-cook time: 3 hours
	Finish time: 10 minutes	Equipment: 5- to 8-quart slow cooker

Recipe on
following page

Spaghetti Pie: Two Ideas

Spaghetti pie is like a cross between a frittata and a casserole—a combination of pasta, eggs, cheese, and seasonings slow-cooked into a crisp-edged pie. It makes a comforting dinner, and it's nice to have leftovers because slices are easily brown-bagged and can be eaten cold, warm, or at room temperature.

Carbonara Spaghetti Pie

There are no peas in a classic carbonara. (Also . . . a classic carbonara is not a pie or made in a slow cooker.) But I love the combination of peas and little bits of crisp, salty pork.

8 ounces *guanciale*, pancetta, or thick-cut bacon, diced

1 pound spaghetti or linguine

7 ounces Parmesan cheese, finely grated (about 2 cups), plus a generous handful for topping

2 cups whole milk or half-and-half

3 large eggs

3 garlic cloves, grated or minced

1½ teaspoons red pepper flakes

Finely grated zest of 1 lemon

1½ teaspoons kosher salt

Freshly ground black pepper

1 cup thawed frozen peas

1. Line a 5- to 7-quart slow cooker with 1 piece of parchment, cut to fit so that it comes up at least 2 inches on all sides (see page xxvi for a how-to). This is to prevent sticking. Bring a large pot of heavily salted water to a boil.

2. Meanwhile, put the *guanciale* (or pork product of your choice) into a dry nonstick skillet and place it over medium heat. Cook until browned and crisped and much of the fat has rendered, 8 to 10 minutes. Remove the *guanciale* with a slotted spoon and drain on paper towels. Reserve the fat.

3. Add the spaghetti to the boiling water, stir, cover the pot to bring it back up to a boil quickly, and then uncover and cook the pasta for 6 to 7 minutes total, until it's floppy but still has a slight crunch in the middle. Drain the pasta and shake it in the colander to cool it down a bit.

4. Meanwhile, in a large bowl, whisk together the Parmesan, milk, eggs, garlic, red pepper flakes, lemon zest, salt, a few generous grinds of black pepper, the crisp *guanciale*, and 2 tablespoons of the reserved pork fat. (If there's less than that, that's fine, just use it all.) Add the drained pasta to the cheese mixture and mix well to coat.

5. Scrape the pasta mixture into the prepared slow cooker and gently pat it into an even cake. Cover and cook on LOW until the pie is set and golden brown around the edges, about 4 hours.

6. Increase the heat to LOW if the slow cooker has auto-switched to warm. Scatter the peas over the pie, cover, and cook for 5 minutes, until just warmed through. Sprinkle the finishing handful of Parmesan over the peas, then cover and cook until softened, 6 minutes. Uncover and let the pie cool for a few minutes. Grabbing the edges of the parchment liner, lift the pie out of the insert.

Holds on warm through step 5 for up to 1 hour	Prep time: 20 minutes	Slow-cook time: 4 hours
	Finish time: 15 minutes	Equipment: 5- to 7-quart slow cooker

See the photo on page 91.

Cacio e Pepe Spaghetti Pie

This peppery, crisp-creamy, cheesy pie was inspired by a recipe by Justin Chapple in Food & Wine.

7 ounces finely grated Parmesan cheese (about 2 cups)

4 ounces grated Gruyère cheese (about 1 cup), plus a generous handful for topping

2 ounces finely grated pecorino Romano cheese (about ¾ cup)

2 cups whole milk or half-and-half

3 large eggs

3 garlic cloves, grated or minced

2 tablespoons olive oil

1½ teaspoons kosher salt

1 tablespoon freshly ground black pepper

1 pound spaghetti or linguine

Chopped fresh flat-leaf parsley, for topping

Lemon wedges, for serving

1. Bring a large pot of heavily salted water to a boil. Meanwhile, in a large bowl, whisk together all three cheeses with the milk, eggs, garlic, oil, salt, and pepper.

2. Line a 5- to 7-quart slow cooker with 1 piece of parchment, cut to fit so that it comes up at least 2 inches on all sides (see page xxvi for a how-to). This is to prevent sticking and also to make it easier to reach in and remove the pie when it's done.

3. Add the spaghetti to the boiling water, stir, and cover the pot to bring it back up to a boil quickly, then uncover the pot and cook the pasta for 6 to 7 minutes total, until it's floppy but still has a slight but noticeable crunch in the middle. Drain the pasta, then shake it in the colander a few times to cool it down a bit. Add the pasta to the bowl with the cheese mixture and mix well to coat.

4. Scrape the pasta mixture into the prepared slow cooker and gently pat it into an even cake. Cover and cook on LOW until the pie is set and golden brown around the edges, about 4 hours.

5. Uncover the slow cooker, add the handful of Gruyère cheese to the top of the pie, and close the lid. Cook until the cheese is melted, about 5 minutes. Uncover and turn off the slow cooker and let the pie rest and cool for a few minutes. Grabbing the edges of the parchment liner, lift the pie out of the insert and set it on a cutting board to rest for at least 5 minutes. Top with the parsley, cut the pie into slices, and serve with lemon wedges on the side.

Holds on warm through step 4 for up to 1 hour	Prep time: 15 minutes	Slow-cook time: 4 hours
	Finish time: 10 minutes	Equipment: 5- to 7-quart slow cooker

Seafood

OIL POACHING

It is easy to use the slow cooker to make infused oils, which can then be used as a flavorful poaching medium. This gentle cooking method is especially good for delicate fish and shellfish, which end up silky and moist. You'll notice that these recipes call for a lot of oil to ensure the ingredients cook evenly, but the oil isn't absorbed into the food in any significant quantity, so the results are not greasy or heavy. You can save the oil to reuse it once more within a week (use it to poach fish again or to make fried rice), but be sure to keep it in the fridge. Be extra careful with the oils that contain garlic, as garlic oil is a botulism risk if it's not refrigerated promptly.

Oniony Poached Salmon with Horseradish Crème Fraîche

Put the salmon and sauce over some arugula simply dressed with olive oil and vinegar to make this a complete meal, or coarsely flake it and put it on a bagel with the crème fraîche sauce.

6 cups (1½ quarts) canola oil

2 medium red onions, quartered

1 lemon, quartered

½ cup crème fraîche

3 tablespoons minced chives

2 tablespoons horseradish, or more to taste

1 tablespoon lemon juice (from about ¼ lemon)

Kosher salt

Four 6- to 8-ounce salmon fillets

1. Combine the oil, onions, and quartered lemon in a 5- to 8-quart slow cooker. Cover and cook on LOW until the oil reaches 200°F on a probe or instant-read thermometer, about 1 hour 30 minutes. (If you'd like to leave this all day, which will make the oil even more flavorful—and make the onions soft and sweet—set your slow cooker to cook on LOW for 1 hour. It can then hold on WARM for up to 7 more hours. When you come home, increase the heat to LOW and let the oil warm to 200°F, which should take 10 to 20 minutes, depending on your slow cooker's temperament.)

2. Meanwhile, combine the crème fraîche, chives, horseradish, and lemon juice in a bowl. Season the sauce with salt. If you want to make it ahead, this sauce will keep well in the fridge for 2 days.

3. Season the salmon with salt and add it to the slow cooker—it's fine for the fillets to overlap, but you want them all to be submerged in the oil as much as possible. Close the lid. Cook for 12 to 15 minutes, depending on how well done you like your salmon. Err on the side of a shorter cook time if you like it translucent in the middle. I find it is perfectly medium-rare when you just see little white beads forming on the outside of the fish. Remove the salmon with a slotted spoon, and if the onions have softened quite a bit (likely if you've left the oil on warm earlier), pull those out to eat, too. (Discard the lemon.) Serve the salmon topped with the sauce.

ALL-DAY	Holds well on warm through step 1 for up to 7 hours	Prep time: 5 minutes	Slow-cook time: About 1 hour 45 minutes
		Finish time: 10 minutes	Equipment: 5- to 8-quart slow cooker

Oil-Poached Shrimp: Two Ideas

Shrimp have a relatively neutral flavor that plays nicely with many different seasonings. Use these ideas as a starting point: Don't have rosemary? You can throw in thyme instead. Feel free to play with what you like and what you have. The flavored oil functions first as a poaching liquid and then as an instant sauce for the shrimp. Try to seek out American-caught wild shrimp or sustainably farmed shrimp. Most of the shrimp you'll find in markets are imported from East Asia or South America, and many come with a host of labor and ecology concerns. For the most up-to-date and detailed information, check Monterey Bay Aquarium's Seafood Watch (Seafoodwatch.org).

Garlic and Rosemary
Oil-Poached Shrimp, 98

Dried Chile and Sichuan
Peppercorn Shrimp, 99

Garlic and Rosemary Oil-Poached Shrimp

MAKES 4 TO 6 SERVINGS

This reminds me of old-school New England Italian-American shrimp scampi, which is usually served with a heap of olive-oiled linguine. You can certainly serve this over pasta— the aromatic oil with lemon juice makes an instant sauce—but I also like it with crusty bread and a simple salad.

When you're done, strain and refrigerate the oil for up to a week. You can use it again to poach or sauté seafood.

6 cups (1½ quarts) extra-virgin olive oil

2 large fresh rosemary sprigs

2 garlic heads, halved crosswise through the equator

1 lemon, quartered

1 teaspoon red pepper flakes

2 pounds large or extra-large shrimp, peeled and deveined

Kosher salt

Chopped fresh flat-leaf parsley, for topping

Lemon wedges, for serving

1. Combine the oil, rosemary, garlic, quartered lemon, and red pepper flakes in a 5- to 8-quart slow cooker. Cover and cook on LOW until the oil reaches 200°F on a probe or instant-read thermometer, about 1 hour 30 minutes. (If you'd like to leave this all day—which will make the oil even more flavorful—set your slow cooker on LOW for 1 hour. It can then hold on WARM for up to 7 more hours. When you come home, increase the heat to LOW and let the oil warm to 200°F, which should take 10 to 20 minutes, depending on your slow cooker's temperament.)

2. Season the shrimp with salt and carefully place them in the oil; close the lid. Cook until the shrimp start to curl and turn opaque, about 12 minutes.

3. Scoop the shrimp and garlic out of the oil with a slotted spoon and toss them together in a serving platter or bowl with a few spoonfuls of the oil. Top with parsley and serve with lemon wedges.

ALL-DAY	Holds well on warm through step 1 for up to 7 hours	Prep time: 10 minutes	Slow-cook time: About 1 hour 45 minutes
		Finish time: 5 minutes	Equipment: 5- to 8-quart slow cooker

See the photo on page 96.

Dried Chile and Sichuan Peppercorn Shrimp

Contrary to what you might guess, this dish is actually relatively mild—it's more floral and aromatic, with a slight warming heat that builds a bit over time. The Sichuan peppercorns add a tingly effect. It's great served warm with rice and sliced cucumber on the side, but my favorite way to eat it is chilled the next day as a light meal or grain-bowl topping.

When you're done, strain and refrigerate the oil for up to a week and use it to make fried rice.

6 cups (1½ quarts) extra-virgin olive oil

20 dried chiles de árbol, broken in half

5 garlic cloves, smashed

¼ cup Sichuan peppercorns

2 pounds large or extra-large shrimp, peeled and deveined

Kosher salt

Chopped fresh cilantro and lime wedges, for serving

1. Combine the oil, chiles, garlic, and peppercorns in a 5- to 8-quart slow cooker. Cover and cook on LOW until the oil reaches 200°F on a probe or instant-read thermometer, about 1 hour 30 minutes. (If you'd like to leave this all day, which will make the oil even more flavorful, set your slow cooker to cook on LOW for 1 hour. It can then hold on WARM for up to 7 more hours. When you come home, increase the heat to LOW and let the oil warm to 200°F, which should take 15 to 20 minutes, depending on your slow cooker's temperament.)

2. Season the shrimp with salt and carefully place them into the oil; close the lid. Cook until the shrimp start to curl and turn opaque, about 12 minutes.

3. Scoop the shrimp and some of the chiles, peppercorns, and garlic out of the oil with a slotted spoon and toss them together in a serving platter or bowl with a few spoonfuls of the oil. (I like to eat the chiles, but most people don't.) Top with cilantro and serve with lime wedges.

Good to know: What you want here are small, dried red chiles. I call for chiles de árbol because I think they are the easiest to find—any grocery store with Latin American ingredients will have them, and so does Amazon, which also carries Sichuan peppercorns. But you can also use any small dried red chiles you find at an Asian market, which might be labeled Thai or Korean or Kashmiri—any of those will work.

ALL-DAY	Holds well on warm through step 1 for up to 7 hours	Prep time: 10 minutes	Slow-cook time: About 1 hour 45 minutes
		Finish time: 5 minutes	Equipment: 5- to 8-quart slow cooker

See the photo on page 97.

Confit with
nder

t even when it's cooked all the way through. Check
od Watch for the most sustainable tuna choices, but
idangered. When the oil has cooled, strain it and
reuse it to poach or sauté fish within about a week.

e oil, garlic, bay leaves, thyme, coriander, and peppercorns
quart slow cooker. Cover and cook on LOW until the oil reach-
a probe or instant-read thermometer, about 1 hour 30 min-
i'd like to leave this all day, set your slow cooker to cook on
ur. It can then hold on WARM for up to 7 more hours. When
ome, increase the heat to LOW and let the oil warm to 200°F,
ld take 10 to 20 minutes, depending on your slow cooker's
nt.)

tuna generously with salt and let it sit at room temperature
matoes cook. Carefully place the tomatoes into the oil, close
cook for 10 minutes. Add the tuna to the slow cooker with
es. Cover and cook for another 10 to 15 minutes, depending
on how well done you like your tuna. (At about 10 minutes the tuna will
have some pink left in the middle; at about 15 minutes the tuna will be
cooked almost all the way through but not dry at all.)

tuna steaks

Kosher salt

12 ounces cherry
tomatoes (about
2 cups)

Freshly ground black
pepper

Lemon wedges, for
serving

3. Scoop the tuna out of the oil and slice against the grain. Scoop the tomatoes and garlic out of the oil with a slotted spoon and toss them together
with the tuna slices in a serving platter or bowl with a few spoonfuls of
the oil. (You can also include a scattering of the oil-poached thyme and
coriander seeds, if you like.) Season everything with pepper and more
salt if necessary. Serve with lemon wedges.

ALL-DAY	Holds well on warm through step 1 for up to 7 hours	Prep time: 10 minutes	Slow-cook time: 1 hour 55 minutes
		Finish time: 5 minutes	Equipment: 5- to 8-quart slow cooker

Lemony Braised Potato Salad with Good Tuna and Arugula

My husband and I can eat almost this entire salad, but if you have more restrained eaters, it could stretch to 4 servings. If you want to bulk it up, braise 2 pounds of potatoes and/or add another can of tuna.

1½ pounds small red or purple potatoes, halved if larger than about 1 inch in diameter

¼ cup lemon juice, plus more for dressing

¼ cup extra-virgin olive oil

5 garlic cloves, crushed

Kosher salt and freshly ground black pepper

Two 6.7-ounce cans good-quality tuna in olive oil, drained

5 ounces arugula (about 5 loosely packed cups)

½ cup pitted kalamata olives

½ small red onion, thinly sliced

1. Combine the potatoes, lemon juice, oil, garlic, 1½ teaspoons salt, a few generous grinds of pepper, and 1 tablespoon water in a 4- to 8-quart slow cooker. Cover and cook until the potatoes are tender, on LOW for about 5 hours or on HIGH for about 2 hours 30 minutes.

2. In a large shallow serving bowl, toss together the tuna, arugula, olives, and onion. Add the warm braised potatoes and some of their braising liquid and toss again to wilt the arugula and evenly combine all the ingredients. Season generously with lemon juice, salt, and pepper.

ALL-DAY	Holds well on warm through step 1 for up to 3 hours	Prep time: 10 minutes	Slow-cook time: 5 hours or 2 hours 30 minutes
		Finish time: 15 minutes	Equipment: 4- to 8-quart slow cooker

Summer Weeknight Shrimp Boil

Here's something to make on a Wednesday in late August when you're tired of tomato salad for dinner. (The slow cooker won't heat up your kitchen.) Maybe a shrimp boil seems like a party— and it can be!—but it can also be an ideal one-pot dinner. Serve the strained ingredients directly on a newspaper-lined table the way traditional shrimp boils are served, or spoon them into individual shallow bowls, including some broth in every serving. Either way, dip crusty bread into the broth, put out a bowl for the shrimp shells, and encourage everyone to eat with their hands.

1 pound small red-skinned potatoes, halved

½ pound smoked Andouille or other smoked sausage, cut into 1-inch slices

¼ cup Old Bay seasoning

Cloves from 1 garlic head, crushed

4 thyme sprigs

12 ounces lager beer, such as Modelo Especial

1 small red or yellow onion, halved

1 lemon, quartered

Kosher salt

2 pounds large or extra-large head-on shrimp

3 ears corn, cut or broken into 4 pieces each

2 tablespoons unsalted butter

Hot sauce to taste (I like a Louisiana-style sauce like Trappey's or Louisiana Brand)

Crusty bread, for serving

1. In a 6- to 8-quart slow cooker, combine the potatoes, sausage, Old Bay seasoning, garlic, thyme, beer, and onion. Squeeze the lemon over everything, then drop the lemon quarters in the cooker, too. Add 4 cups water and ½ teaspoon salt. Cover and cook on LOW until the potatoes are tender, about 5 hours.

2. Using a slotted spoon, discard the lemon quarters and onion halves. Increase the heat to HIGH. Add the shrimp and corn on the cob, stirring gently to mix. Cook until the shrimp are just opaque all the way through, 12 to 18 minutes, depending on their size and the temperament of your slow cooker.

3. Stir in the butter and as much hot sauce as you like. Taste the broth and season it with more salt if it tastes flat. Serve in individual bowls or use a slotted spoon to pile the ingredients on a newspaper-lined table, with bowls of broth on the side and bread for dipping.

Good to know: Head-on shrimp are a treat: There's deep flavor in those heads and shells that makes the broth extra delicious. You will not regret seeking them out, but this recipe will also work with any shrimp you find in your market. Shelled shrimp will cook more quickly, in around 12 minutes, so keep an eye on them.

ALL-DAY	Holds well on warm through step 1 for up to 3 hours	Prep time: 15 minutes	Slow-cook time: 5 hours 20 minutes
		Finish time: 5 minutes	Equipment: 6- to 8-quart slow cooker

Vegetarian

Ricotta-Spinach Polenta with Tomato Salad

MAKES 4 SERVINGS

Polenta is often used as a neutral carb canvas for a rich sauce or braised meat, but here the creamy ricotta-and-spinach-enriched polenta is the centerpiece, with a simple little tomato salad on top for freshness. An egg on top is great, but optional.

1½ cups polenta (not instant or quick-cooking)

2 tablespoons unsalted butter, cut into bits

Kosher salt

5 ounces baby spinach (about 5 loosely packed cups)

1 pint cherry tomatoes, halved

2 teaspoons extra-virgin olive oil, plus more for the eggs

2 teaspoons balsamic vinegar

Freshly ground black pepper

4 large eggs (optional)

1 cup grated Parmesan

1 cup whole or part-skim milk ricotta

1. Combine the polenta with 6½ cups water in a 5- to 7-quart slow cooker. Add the butter and 2 teaspoons salt. Cover and cook on LOW until the polenta is thick and tender, about 6 hours.

2. With the slow cooker on LOW, stir the polenta well and then stir the spinach into the polenta in 2 batches, covering the cooker and letting the first batch wilt before adding the second, about 5 minutes per batch.

3. Meanwhile, in a medium bowl, toss together the tomatoes, oil, and vinegar. Season the tomato salad with salt and pepper.

4. Optional: Pour a thin layer of oil into a large skillet over medium-high heat and crack 4 eggs into the pan. Season the eggs with salt and pepper and cook until the whites are golden brown, lacy on the edges, and just set in the middle, and the yolks are still a little jiggly, about 3 minutes.

5. Fold the Parmesan and ricotta into the polenta. Taste and season the polenta with salt if necessary. Stir in warm water by the tablespoon if the polenta is looking too thick for your taste—keep in mind it will continue to thicken as it cools. Top bowls of the polenta with the tomato salad and, if you like, the fried eggs.

Good to know: If you're cooking for strict vegetarians, don't use imported Parmesan (the good stuff!) because it's probably made with animal rennet. Instead, seek out a domestic "parmesan" (the okay stuff) that's labeled vegetarian, like the one made by BelGioioso.

| ALL-DAY | Holds well on warm through step 1 for up to 3 hours | Prep time: 5 minutes | Slow-cook time: 6 hours |
| | | Finish time: 20 minutes | Equipment: 5- to 7-quart slow cooker |

Dal with Mango and Mustard Seeds

MAKES 6 SERVINGS

My mother-in-law is a truly great, intuitive cook—every single thing that comes out of her kitchen is mind-blowingly delicious. She's a doctor who grew up in Mumbai and cooks mainly Indian food from her home state of Maharashtra. It's different from the Northern Indian food you find at most Indian restaurants in the United States—lighter and brighter, with lots of seafood and vegetables. She doesn't use recipes; instead, she just tastes as she goes. This is my unauthorized-biography-style, very imperfect re-creation of her dal.

1 pound dried red lentils

One 10-ounce bag frozen mango chunks

Kosher salt

4 tablespoons canola oil

1 yellow or red onion, finely chopped

3 large garlic cloves, grated or minced

One 2-inch ginger knob, peeled and grated or minced (about 2 tablespoons)

1 tablespoon garam masala

2 teaspoons mustard seeds

1 teaspoon red pepper flakes, or to taste

1 teaspoon ground turmeric

2 cups mango nectar, plus more to taste

2 teaspoons cumin seeds

Plain yogurt and chopped fresh cilantro, for topping

Lime wedges, for serving

1. Stir together the lentils, mango, and 1 tablespoon kosher salt in a 5- to 8-quart slow cooker.

2. Warm 3 tablespoons of the oil in a skillet over medium-high heat. Add the onion, season with salt, and cook, stirring, until the onion is softened and golden, about 8 minutes. Reduce the heat to medium and stir in the garlic and ginger. Cook, stirring, for a minute or so. Stir in the garam masala, mustard seeds, red pepper flakes, and turmeric. Cook, stirring constantly, for about 2 minutes, until very fragrant and well combined. Pour in 2 cups water, stir and scrape the bottom of the pan to make sure any toasted spices and browned bits of onion get incorporated, and pour the whole thing into the slow cooker. Add 4 more cups water and the mango nectar. Stir everything together, cover, and cook on LOW until the flavors mellow and the lentils are soupy and tender, about 9 hours.

3. When you're ready to serve, stir the dal well and check it for consistency and seasoning. Add more water or mango nectar if it's too thick or too spicy, and add salt and/or red pepper flakes if it's tasting flat.

4. Warm the remaining 1 tablespoon oil in a small saucepan over medium-high heat and add the cumin seeds. Let them pop and crackle and get really fragrant for 30 seconds or so, stirring to make sure they don't burn. Tip the oil and cumin seeds into the dal and stir to combine. Serve in bowls topped with yogurt and cilantro and with lime wedges on the side.

Good to know: I call for frozen mango here because it's so much better (and easier) to use good frozen mango than a mediocre, fibrous, out-of-season fresh mango. But if you have a couple great mangoes (look for Ataúlfo or Champagne varieties from Mexico), please go ahead and throw them in instead.

ALL-DAY	Holds well on warm through step 2 for up to 2 hours	Prep time: 20 minutes	Slow-cook time: 9 hours
		Finish time: 5 minutes	Equipment: 5- to 8-quart slow cooker

Shakshuka with Feta and Olives

MAKES 2 TO 4 SERVINGS

This is a simple and comforting North African dish of eggs cooked in a spicy tomato and red pepper sauce. The sauce is very forgiving and can hold on warm for a long time, so it's one of my favorite weeknight dinners when you don't know exactly when you'll be home.

3 tablespoons extra-virgin olive oil, plus more for serving

1 large red or yellow onion, sliced

Kosher salt

12 ounces jarred roasted red peppers, drained and sliced (about 1 heaping cup)

One 28-ounce can whole tomatoes

½ cup pitted olives, preferably kalamata

5 garlic cloves, chopped

½ teaspoon ground cumin

½ teaspoon ground turmeric

½ teaspoon smoked paprika

½ teaspoon red pepper flakes

1 tablespoon *schug* or harissa (see note, below), plus more to taste

Freshly ground black pepper

4 large eggs

Fresh herbs, such as parsley, mint, or dill, and feta, for topping

Pita bread, for serving

1. Warm the oil in a medium skillet over medium-high heat. Add the onion, season it with salt, and cook, stirring occasionally, until the onion softens and starts to turn golden, 8 minutes.

2. Meanwhile, put the roasted red peppers, tomatoes, and olives into a 5- to 8-quart slow cooker. With your hands, coarsely break up the tomatoes.

3. Add the garlic to the skillet with the onions, season with salt, and cook, stirring, for 2 minutes. Lower the heat to medium and add the cumin, turmeric, paprika, red pepper flakes, and *schug*. Season generously with pepper. Cook, stirring, until fragrant and combined, about 30 seconds. Using a spatula, scrape the onion mixture into the slow cooker (be sure to include the oil) and stir to combine. Season with 1 teaspoon salt. Cook on LOW until the sauce's flavors have married and mellowed, 6 to 8 hours. (You could also cook this on HIGH for 2 hours 30 minutes to 3 hours.)

4. Taste the sauce and add salt and more *schug* if you like. Turn the heat up to HIGH, cover, and wait for the edges to start bubbling slightly, about 15 minutes. Stir the sauce, then crack the eggs onto the surface of the sauce and season them with a little salt. Cover and cook for 8 to 15 more minutes, until the eggs are just set on top (which is where they cook slowest) but still jiggly. Scoop servings into bowls and drizzle with a little olive oil. Top with the herbs and feta and serve with pita on the side.

Good to know: Schug *(also spelled* zhug*) is a Yemenite hot sauce that's popular in Israel. It's tangy and hot and herbal and comes in both red and green varieties; either will work here. Look for it in your supermarket near the hummus—Sabra makes a very good jarred version. But if you can't find it, harissa (see note, page 124) will also be excellent.*

ALL-DAY	Holds well on warm through step 3 for up to 4 hours	Prep time: 15 minutes	Slow-cook time: 6 to 8 hours
		Finish time: 30 minutes	Equipment: 5- to 8-quart slow cooker

Eggplant: Two Ideas

Eggplant gets silky and tender with long, gentle heat. Add assertive flavors and a ready-to-go protein—such as chickpeas or smoked tofu—and it's a natural weeknight dinner.

Harissa-and-Honey-Braised Eggplant with Chickpeas

MAKES 2 MAIN COURSE OR 4 SIDE DISH SERVINGS

After you braise the eggplants, you have the option to broil them. I like the way this concentrates their flavor and adds a little smoky, charred flourish. But if you're in a real rush, you can skip that step.

1½ to 2 pounds small to medium eggplants, such as Japanese or Graffiti eggplants, or very small Italian eggplants

¼ cup harissa (see note, page 124), plus more if necessary

¼ cup extra-virgin olive oil

2 tablespoons honey, plus more if necessary

Juice of ½ lemon

Kosher salt

1½ cups Basic Slow-Cooked Chickpeas (page 13) or one 15-ounce can chickpeas, drained and rinsed

Plain yogurt and/or crumbled feta cheese and chopped fresh flat-leaf parsley, for topping

1. Leaving the stem ends of the eggplants completely intact, cut each eggplant into lengthwise quarters by making 2 perpendicular slices up from the bottom of the eggplant to the stem (but not through it); this way, the eggplant stays together but the flesh is separated into 4 quadrants, almost like the petals of a flower.

2. Combine the harissa, oil, honey, lemon juice, and 1½ teaspoons salt in a 5- to 8-quart slow cooker. Add the eggplants and rub the seasoning all over them, including inside the cut pieces, so that all the exposed flesh is stained red. Cover and cook on LOW until the eggplants are slumped and very tender, 5 to 6 hours.

3. Optional step: Preheat the broiler on high and position a rack 6 inches below the heat source (if that's how your broiler works). Line a baking sheet with parchment paper. Carefully remove the eggplants from the slow cooker with a slotted spoon or tongs (leave the juices in there) and place them on the prepared baking sheet. Broil until caramelized and slightly charred in spots, 3 to 5 minutes. Return the eggplants to the slow cooker.

4. Pick up here if you have skipped the broiling step: With the slow cooker on WARM, toss in the chickpeas, cover, and cook until the chickpeas are just warmed through, 3 to 5 minutes. Taste and add more salt, harissa, or honey if needed. Serve in bowls topped with yogurt or feta and parsley.

ALL-DAY	Holds on warm through step 2 for up to 3 hours	Prep time: 10 minutes	Slow-cook time: 5 to 6 hours
		Finish time: 10 minutes	Equipment: 5- to 8-quart slow cooker

Chinese Chile-Bean Eggplant with Smoked Tofu

MAKES 2 MAIN COURSE OR 4 SIDE DISH SERVINGS

This dish is rich, earthy, and spicy thanks to the toban djan, *or chile and fermented bean paste, which pairs deliciously with eggplant. You can find smoked or baked tofu in the refrigerated section of most large grocery stores—it's ready to eat and just needs to be warmed through.*

As in the previous recipe, after you braise the eggplants, you have the option to broil them. I like the way this concentrates their flavor and adds a little smoky, charred flourish. But if you're in a real rush, you can skip that step.

1½ to 2 pounds medium to small eggplants, such as Japanese or Graffiti eggplants, or very small Italian eggplants

¼ cup canola oil

¼ cup Chinese chile-bean sauce (*toban djan*) or Chinese black bean sauce, plus more if necessary (these are different products but either will work; see note, opposite)

2 tablespoons packed light brown sugar, plus more if necessary

Kosher salt

6 ounces smoked or baked tofu, cut into bite-size pieces

Juice of ½ lime

2 scallions, trimmed and thinly sliced, for topping

Rice, for serving (about 1 cooked cup per person; optional)

1. Leaving the stem ends of the eggplants completely intact, cut each eggplant into lengthwise quarters by making 2 perpendicular slices up from the bottom of the eggplant to the stem (but not through it); this way, the eggplant stays together but the flesh is separated into 4 quadrants, almost like the petals of a flower.

2. Combine the oil, chile-bean sauce, sugar, and a pinch of salt in a 5- to 8-quart slow cooker. Add the eggplants and rub the seasoning all over them, including inside the cut pieces, so that all the exposed flesh is stained red from the seasoning. Cover and cook on LOW until the eggplants are slumped and very tender, 5 to 6 hours.

3. Optional step: Preheat the broiler on high. Line a baking sheet with parchment paper. Carefully remove the eggplants from the slow cooker with a slotted spoon or tongs (leave the juices in there) and place them on the prepared baking sheet. Broil until caramelized and slightly charred in spots, 3 to 5 minutes.

4. Pick up here if you have skipped the broiling step: Return the eggplants to the slow cooker. With the slow cooker on WARM, toss in the smoked tofu, cover, and let sit until just warmed through, 3 to 5 minutes. Squeeze in the lime juice. Taste and add more salt, chile-bean paste, or brown sugar if you like. Serve in bowls topped with the scallions and, if desired, with cooked rice on the side.

Good to know: Toban djan (*also spelled* doubanjiang) *is a Sichuan-style fermented bean and chile sauce. The one most available in American supermarkets is made by Lee Kum Kee—but it's also worth seeking out other brands, especially those made in Sichuan province. Find them in Chinese groceries, the Mala Market (themalamarket.com), and on Amazon. Black bean sauce is a completely different product but also has a fermented bean base and is just as delicious with eggplant. Lee Kum Kee also makes a version that is common in large supermarkets.*

ALL-DAY	Holds on warm through step 2 for up to 3 hours	Prep time: 10 minutes	Slow-cook time: 5 to 6 hours
		Finish time: 10 minutes	Equipment: 5- to 8-quart slow cooker

Tarragon Beets, 118

Ricotta Tartines: Three Ideas

Most people associate the slow cooker with braised meat, but it can also braise vegetables beautifully. Because they give off moisture as they cook, the vegetables' cooking liquid doubles as a flavorful sauce. Here are three ideas—for beets, cherry tomatoes, and fennel with shallot. Make them into a full dinner by turning them into open-faced ricotta sandwiches (or fabulous grain-bowl toppings). These three ideas take you from summer to fall to winter.

Olive Oil–Braised
Fennel and Shallot, 119

Caramelized Cherry
Tomatoes, 119

Vegetable Ricotta Tartines

4 thick slices good crusty bread, toasted

8 ounces whole milk ricotta

Kosher salt and freshly ground black pepper

Tarragon Beets, Caramelized Cherry Tomatoes, or Olive Oil–Braised Fennel and Shallot (recipes follow), for topping

Thickly spread the toasts with ricotta and season them with salt and pepper. Top the ricotta with beets, tomatoes, or fennel and shallot and drizzle the tartines with the vegetables' sauce.

TARRAGON BEETS

Scrub and trim 4 medium-large **beets** (about 1 pound), but don't peel them. Put the beets into a 4- to 8-quart slow cooker and season them generously with 2 big pinches of **kosher salt**. Add 2 tablespoons **olive oil** and stir to coat. Cook until the beets are tender when you test them with the tip of a knife, about 3 hours on HIGH or 5 hours on LOW. (These will hold well on WARM for up to 1 hour.) Remove the beets (reserve the cooking liquid in the slow cooker) and let them cool enough to handle. Peel the skin from the beets with your hands (they should come off easily) and thinly slice them. (Wear gloves if you don't want to stain your hands.) Put them into a bowl and pour their cooking liquid over them. Add 2 teaspoons **olive oil** and the juice of 1 **lemon**. Add 2 teaspoons chopped fresh **tarragon** and 1 trimmed, sliced **scallion**. Toss and season to taste with **kosher salt** and **freshly ground black pepper**. Store the beets in an airtight container in the refrigerator for up to 3 days; they are good cold, hot, or at room temperature.

See the photo on page 116.

CARAMELIZED CHERRY TOMATOES

Combine 2 pints (about 1 pound or 3 loose cups) **cherry tomatoes**, 2 tablespoons **olive oil**, 1 tablespoon **honey**, 2 **thyme** sprigs, and 1 teaspoon **kosher salt** in a 4- to 7-quart slow cooker. Stir to combine all the ingredients and set the lid ajar so that there's a 1- to 2-inch gap. (This will allow the tomato juices to reduce and caramelize.) Cook on LOW until the tomatoes are sweet and caramelized, many of them have burst, and their juices are sticky, about 7 hours, stirring occasionally if you can. (This will keep well on WARM for up to 1 hour.) Remove the thyme sprigs and stir in ½ teaspoon chopped fresh **thyme** leaves. Add 1 teaspoon **balsamic vinegar** or more to taste. Season to taste with **kosher salt** and **freshly ground black pepper**. Store the tomatoes in the refrigerator for up to 3 days; they are good cold, hot, or at room temperature.

OLIVE OIL–BRAISED FENNEL AND SHALLOT

Start with 1 large or 2 small **fennel bulbs** (about 1½ pounds total). Cut off the delicate, feathery green fronds and reserve them for later. Cut the fennel bulb in half, core it, and then slice both the bulb and the stalks crosswise (against the grain) into ½-inch- to 1-inch-thick pieces. Put the pieces into a 5- to 8-quart slow cooker. Add 5 halved small **shallots** (6 to 8 ounces), ½ cup **olive oil**, 2 teaspoons **apple cider vinegar**, 1 teaspoon **kosher salt**, and ½ teaspoon **red pepper flakes**. Stir to combine all the ingredients. Cover and cook on LOW until the fennel and shallots are tender and sweet, 8 to 10 hours, stirring once or twice if possible. (This holds well on WARM for up to 2 hours.) Stir in the **reserved fennel fronds** and 2 teaspoons **apple cider vinegar**. Season to taste with **kosher salt** and **freshly ground black pepper**. Store the fennel and shallots in the refrigerator for up to 3 days; they are good cold, hot, or at room temperature.

See the photos on page 117.

Pork, Lamb, and Beef

Recipe on page 122

Meatballs: Two Ideas

The slow cooker can effortlessly handle certain dishes that few people think of as slow-cooker staples, like custards and congee, polenta and risotto, pho and tamales. And then there are a lot of dishes that seem like slow-cooker naturals, which actually need some extra thought and attention to work— like meatballs. Meatballs are great made in the slow cooker. But if you leave them in there too long, even on the warm setting, they will eventually give up all their delicious juices and dry out. (The sauce will be extra-delicious, because that's where the juices went.) To guard against this, I've added lots of moisture-lending ingredients, like buttermilk and an extra egg yolk. The meatballs here are best if you can take them off the heat after four hours. Leaving them on warm for a couple hours longer isn't going to do much harm, but they will slowly lose their juiciness. Longer than about seven hours total will make them noticeably dry.

Also, you'll notice I haven't browned the meatballs before cooking them. Browning has advantages: It renders some of the fat, so that the fat doesn't end up in your sauce (though some fat is delicious), and it gives the meatballs extra flavor and texture. But I also think it jump-starts the cooking process and makes it impossible to leave the meatballs in the slow cooker as long as many people find most convenient. However, if you'd like, put the meatballs on a parchment- or foil-lined baking sheet and run them under the broiler for about five minutes per side, flipping them once, for a total of about ten minutes. Then, using tongs, add them to the slow cooker and cut the cook time to two or three hours, checking the internal temperature with an instant-read thermometer.

Italian Deli Mozzarella-Stuffed Meatballs in Lots of Sauce

These meatballs channel the punchy, bright flavors of an Italian-American deli sub. Using good-quality hot Italian sausage is a huge time-saver here: It has assertive seasonings like chile, garlic, and herbs, so that you don't need to add a lot of other ingredients to get a flavorful result. I round out the sausage with ground chicken or turkey, which are usually too lean on their own but make a perfect combination when mixed 50/50 with fatty sausage.

You'll end up with a lot of sauce—almost like a thick tomato broth, rich with sausage juices. Serve the sauce-smothered meatballs (one or two, at most, per person) in shallow bowls with crusty bread for mopping.

1 onion, garlic, or kaiser roll (2 to 2.5 ounces)

⅓ cup buttermilk

One 28-ounce can crushed tomatoes, preferably fire-roasted

¼ cup sliced, drained *peperoncini*, cherry, or banana peppers

Kosher salt and freshly ground black pepper

1 pound ground chicken or turkey

1 pound raw hot Italian sausage, squeezed out of its casing

1. Tear the roll into small bits and put the pieces into a medium bowl. Pour the buttermilk over the top, mix it to combine, and set aside while you prepare the other ingredients.

2. Put the tomatoes into a 6- to 8-quart slow cooker and stir in the *peperoncini*. Add ½ teaspoon salt and a generous grind of pepper.

3. In a large bowl, combine the ground chicken, sausage, spinach, beaten egg and yolk, parsley, oregano, red pepper flakes, 1 teaspoon salt, and a few generous grinds of pepper.

4. Now that the roll has been sitting in the buttermilk for a few minutes, it should be softened. With your hands, mush the roll into the buttermilk until the roll disintegrates and you have a uniform goop. Add this to the bowl with the meat and mix everything with your hands until it is fully combined.

One 10-ounce package
frozen chopped
spinach, thawed and
very thoroughly wrung
dry

1 large egg plus 1 large
egg yolk, lightly
beaten

¼ cup chopped fresh
flat-leaf parsley

1 teaspoon dried
oregano

1 teaspoon red pepper
flakes

8 or 9 marinated (or
plain) *ciliegine* or
bocconcini (small
fresh mozzarella balls)

Crusty bread, for
serving

5. Take a small handful of the mixture and flatten it slightly in your palm. Put 1 mozzarella ball on top, then take another small handful of the meat mixture, flatten it slightly, and put it on top of the cheese. Now pinch and pat the meat mixture together to form a ball that fully encloses the cheese inside. It should be about the size of a very small apple or a baseball (but not as big as a softball). Put the meatball into the sauce in the slow cooker and repeat with the remaining mixture to form 8 or 9 meatballs total, nestling the meatballs next to each other in the slow cooker as you go. (It will be crowded, but they should all fit.) Cook on **LOW** for 4 hours, or until the internal temperature is at least 160°F when you check the middle of a meatball with an instant-read thermometer. (Or, better yet, stick a probe thermometer in a meatball before you start cooking so you can monitor the internal temperature without lifting the lid.)

6. Remove the meatballs from the sauce with a slotted spoon and put them into a shallow serving bowl. If there is visible fat on the top of the sauce, skim it off, and then taste the sauce and adjust the seasoning if you like. Add the sauce to the meatballs in the bowl. Serve with bread on the side.

Good to know: Bocconcini are two-bite-size fresh mozzarella balls and ciliegine are one-bite, cherry-size balls. Either will work here. Best of all, use ciliegine or bocconcini that are marinated in herbs and olive oil—they are available at some grocery stores, Italian markets, or really anywhere that sells antipasti. But the unmarinated versions are great, too, and regular fresh mozzarella will work just fine as well—you'll just have to take the time to cube it into bite-size pieces.

Holds well on warm through step 5 for a maximum of 3 hours	Prep time: 30 minutes	Slow-cook time: 4 hours
	Finish time: 5 minutes	Equipment: 6- to 8-quart slow cooker

Spiced Lamb Meatballs in Harissa Tomato Sauce

MAKES 3 TO 4 SERVINGS

This combination of flavors—rich lamb, punchy harissa, warm spices—is one of my absolute favorites. The addition of spinach makes it a well-rounded meal, but you could skip the spinach entirely, or use another tender, quick-cooking green, such as arugula or baby kale.

1 pound ground lamb

½ cup panko or toasted bread crumbs

1 large egg plus 1 egg yolk, beaten

1 scallion, trimmed and thinly sliced, or 3 tablespoons grated yellow or red onion

½ teaspoon ground cumin

½ teaspoon red pepper flakes

1. Gently combine the lamb, bread crumbs, beaten egg and yolk, scallion, cumin, red pepper flakes, cinnamon, mint, lemon zest, garlic, and ¾ teaspoon salt in a large bowl. The best way to do this is with your hands—you want everything to be thoroughly mixed but not overmixed, which makes for tough meatballs.

2. Put the tomatoes and harissa into a 5- to 8-quart slow cooker. With your hands or a fork, break up the tomatoes a little, but don't worry about leaving some big chunks. Season the sauce with 1 teaspoon salt.

3. Form the meat mixture into meatballs a little bigger than a golf ball, about 8 meatballs total. Put them into the sauce and turn once to coat.

A Note about Harissa

You might notice that I use a lot of harissa—a North African spice paste made of various peppers, olive oil, and garlic—especially in weeknight dinner recipes. That's because I find it incredibly convenient: a spicy-but-not-too-spicy, garlicky-but-not-too-garlicky flavor boost that pairs beautifully with Middle Eastern– and Mediterranean-inspired dishes. You can find it in cans, tubes, and jars, and though different brands may vary in texture and heat level, any harissa you find will work in these recipes. Just taste it first to see how spicy it is and feel free to modify the quantity called for to suit your taste. You can find harissa in some grocery stores or on Amazon. My very favorite harissa brand, the best I have ever tasted, is made by New York Shuk (www.nyshuk.com), a small company run by an Israeli couple who now live and cook in New York. Their homemade harissa is a splurge, but it's worth it.

½ teaspoon ground cinnamon

¼ cup finely chopped fresh mint or flat-leaf parsley, plus more for topping

Finely grated zest of ½ lemon or 1 lime

2 garlic cloves, grated or finely minced

Kosher salt

One 28-ounce can whole tomatoes

3 tablespoons harissa (see note, opposite), plus more for seasoning

5 ounces baby spinach (about 5 loosely packed cups; optional)

Polenta (about 1 cooked cup per person; page 9) or crusty bread, for serving

Cook on LOW for 4 hours, or until the internal temperature is at least 160°F when you check the middle of a meatball with an instant-read thermometer. (Or, better yet, stick a probe thermometer in a meatball before you start cooking so you can monitor the internal temperature without lifting the lid.)

4. Increase the heat to LOW if the slow cooker has auto-switched to warm. Stir in the spinach, if using, and cover and cook until wilted, about 8 minutes. Taste the sauce and stir in more harissa or salt if you want. Ladle the meatballs and sauce into bowls, top them with additional herbs, and serve them with polenta or bread.

Holds well on warm through step 3 for a maximum of 3 hours	Prep time: 15 minutes	Slow-cook time: 4 hours
	Finish time: 10 minutes	Equipment: 5- to 8-quart slow cooker

Smoky "Barbecued" Brisket

This recipe is adapted from Floyd Cardoz's wonderful cookbook One Spice, Two Spice. *Cardoz uses spices in incredibly smart, unexpected combinations. This brisket, which Cardoz makes in the oven and I've rejiggered for the slow cooker, is vaguely reminiscent of classic Southern barbecue, but the sauce is deeper and more complex, almost bitter-edged but in a pleasant way. It gets its smokiness from the pasilla de Oaxaca chiles.*

2 dried pasilla de Oaxaca chiles

1 white onion, roughly chopped

8 garlic cloves, smashed

One 3-inch ginger knob, peeled and roughly chopped (about 3 tablespoons)

¼ cup apple cider vinegar

3 tablespoons packed light brown sugar

2 tablespoons tomato paste

1 tablespoon red pepper flakes

1 tablespoon mustard seeds

1. Put the dried chiles into a dry skillet over medium-high heat and toast, pressing them into the pan every now and then, and flipping them a few times, until they soften slightly and are fragrant, 2 to 3 minutes.

2. Tear the chiles into pieces, discarding the stems and most of the seeds, and put the pieces into a blender. Add the onion, garlic, ginger, vinegar, sugar, tomato paste, red pepper flakes, mustard seeds, cumin, turmeric, cloves, and a generous pinch of salt. Pour in about half the beer, just enough to make it easy to puree the ingredients but not so much that it will foam over the top of the blender. Puree until smooth, stopping to stir, scrape down the blender, and add more beer if necessary.

3. Pour the pureed sauce into a 5- to 8-quart slow cooker. Pour the rest of the beer into the blender and swish it around to loosen any sauce that's sticking to the sides. Pour it into the slow cooker and add the cinnamon sticks. Pat the brisket dry and season it very generously on both sides with salt. Add it to the slow cooker and turn to coat it in the sauce. Cover and cook on LOW until tender, about 8 hours.

1½ teaspoons ground cumin

1 teaspoon ground turmeric

¼ teaspoon ground cloves

Kosher salt

12 ounces Belgian ale or crisp pilsner, such as Duvel ale or Jever pilsner

2 cinnamon sticks

2 pounds brisket, excess fat trimmed

Corn bread, for serving

4. Remove the brisket with tongs and let it rest on a cutting board for a few minutes. Slice the brisket against the grain, place on a serving platter, and smother it with sauce. Serve with corn bread on the side.

Good to know: You can buy pasillas de Oaxaca at some Latin American markets or at worldspice.com. They are smokier, fruitier, and less hot than chipotles, but if you can't find the pasillas, you can substitute 2 or 3 chipotles, either dried or from a can of chipotles in adobo. If you use the canned chiles, skip step 1 and just put the whole chiles in the blender.

ALL-DAY	Holds well on warm through step 3 for up to 3 hours	Prep time: 20 minutes	Slow-cook time: 8 hours
		Finish time: 5 minutes	Equipment: 5- to 8-quart slow cooker and a blender

Spicy Kimchi and Pork Ramen

This is one of my very favorite weeknight meals—the stew has a rich, complex depth of flavor thanks to the gochujang, a Korean chile paste made with fermented soybeans and glutinous rice. It renders everything it touches completely delicious.

It might seem fussy, but I add the kimchi in 2 batches here for a reason: As it cooks, the pickled cabbage gets mellow and sweet. Then, at the end, you stir in the last ½ cup of kimchi to get the bright, tangy note that's been nearly cooked out of the first batch.

One 16-ounce jar napa cabbage kimchi, chopped (about 2 cups chopped kimchi and 3 tablespoons kimchi juice)

1 pound boneless pork shoulder, trimmed of excess fat and cut into 2-inch chunks

½ cup *gochujang*, plus more to taste

1. Set aside ½ cup of the chopped kimchi in the refrigerator. Combine the remaining kimchi and its juice with the pork, *gochujang*, soy sauce, sugar, fish sauce, and 8 cups water in a 5- to 8-quart slow cooker. Cover and cook until the pork is very tender, 8 to 9 hours on LOW.

2. Shred the meat with 2 forks if you'd like, or leave it in chunks. Stir in the reserved kimchi. Taste for seasoning.

Recipe continues on page 130.

Soft- or Medium-Boiled Eggs

Bring a large saucepan of water to a rolling boil over high heat. Carefully drop in 4 to 6 eggs and boil for 6 minutes for completely liquid yolks or 8 minutes for medium yolks. Immediately transfer the eggs to a bowl of ice water using a slotted spoon. Peel and eat or store unpeeled eggs in the refrigerator for up to a week.

2 tablespoons soy sauce

2 tablespoons packed light brown sugar or raw sugar

1 tablespoon fish sauce

16 ounces dried or fresh ramen noodles, cooked to package directions and drained

4 soft- or medium-boiled eggs, halved (see note, page 128)

2 scallions, trimmed and thinly sliced on the diagonal, for topping

Sliced nori seaweed, for topping

3. Divide the cooked noodles among 4 bowls and ladle the soup on top. Gently place 1 halved egg into each bowl, sprinkle scallions and nori on top, and serve.

Good to know: You can find gochujang at Korean groceries or on Amazon. Look for the wonderful Mother-in-Law's brand, which offers several different varieties—like tangy, sesame, and garlic.

ALL-DAY	Holds well on warm through step 1 for up to 3 hours	Prep time: 10 minutes	Slow-cook time: 8 to 9 hours
		Finish time: 10 minutes	Equipment: 5- to 8-quart slow cooker

Italian Wedding Soup with Sausage Meatballs and Kale

MAKES 4 TO 6 SERVINGS

This is an excellent way to showcase the rich, deep flavor of Parmesan-Garlic Broth (page 4). You can use any kind of raw sausage that you like here—sweet or hot Italian pork or turkey sausage is great, but so is a broccoli rabe sausage if you can find it. (If you'd rather use fully cooked sausage, just slice it into coins, add them to the soup, and let them warm through.)

2 tablespoons olive oil

1 large yellow or red onion, diced

Kosher salt

4 large garlic cloves, chopped

2 large carrots, sliced

1 fennel bulb, cored and thinly sliced, fronds reserved for serving

Freshly ground black pepper

8 cups Parmesan-Garlic Broth (page 4), Classic Chicken Stock (page 5), or low-sodium chicken broth

1 pound raw Italian sausage, squeezed out of its casing

1 bunch of kale (8 to 10 ounces), stemmed and chopped

Juice of ½ lemon, plus more if necessary

Chopped fresh flat-leaf parsley and grated Parmesan, for topping

1. Warm the oil in a large skillet over medium-high heat. Add the onion, season generously with salt, and cook, stirring occasionally, until softened and lightly golden, 8 minutes. Add the garlic, carrots, and fennel, season again with salt, and cook until the vegetables are just softened, about 3 minutes. Season generously with pepper and scrape the vegetable mixture into a 5- to 8-quart slow cooker. Pour in the broth. If your broth is unsalted, add ½ teaspoon salt. (If it is salted, don't add more salt right now.) Cover and cook on LOW for 7 hours.

2. Increase the heat to HIGH. Roll the sausage into bite-size meatballs and drop them into the slow cooker. Stir in the kale and the lemon juice. Cover and cook until the sausage is cooked through and the kale is tender, about 30 minutes.

3. Taste and add more salt, pepper, and lemon juice if you like. Serve the soup in bowls topped with the reserved fennel fronds, the parsley, and grated Parmesan.

ALL-DAY	Holds well on warm through step 1 or step 2 for up to 2 hours	Prep time: 15 minutes	Slow-cook time: 7 hours
		Finish time: 35 minutes	Equipment: 5- to 8-quart slow cooker

See the photo on pages 132-133.

Italian Wedding Soup with
Sausage Meatballs and Kale, 131

Chipotle-Almond Braised Beef Tacos

This sauce is inspired by mole, the various fruit, nut, and chile-based sauces that are famously made in a rainbow of colors and flavors in Mexico, particularly Oaxaca state. This is my quickie, weeknight version that is not at all authentic but does have a complex savory-spicy-sweet flavor that is very reminiscent of proper moles. I've borrowed the pureed nuts, seeds, tortillas, and fruit from more traditional recipes—those ingredients lend richness and depth—and added convenient canned chipotles in adobo for smokiness and heat and Nutella for an almost imperceptible hint of sweetness and cocoa.

Braising the beef directly in the sauce seems like the natural thing to do, but the sauce loses its vibrancy when cooked for a long time. Cooking the beef separately and then tossing it with the sauce lets the beef get a nice brown crust and the sauce stay flavorful.

3½ pounds beef chuck roast, trimmed of big hunks of fat and cut into 2 big pieces (you can also use lamb or goat shoulder)

Kosher salt

1 corn tortilla, plus more warmed tortillas, about 2 per person, for serving

2 tablespoons canola oil

2 garlic cloves, smashed

½ tart apple, such as Granny Smith, peeled, cored, and chopped

½ white onion, chopped

¼ cup raisins

2 tablespoons sesame seeds

1½ teaspoons coriander seeds

1. Put the beef into a 5- to 8-quart slow cooker and season it very generously on all sides with salt. Cover and cook on LOW until the beef is tender, 8 to 10 hours.

2. Make the sauce: If you have a gas stove, put the tortilla directly over a burner set to medium. Let the tortilla get soft and charred in spots, about 30 seconds per side. Tear the tortilla into pieces and put the pieces into a food processor or blender. (If you don't have a gas stove, just put the torn tortilla into the food processor or blender.)

3. Warm the oil in a large skillet over medium-high heat and add the garlic, apple, and onion. Season generously with salt and cook, stirring occasionally, until softened and starting to brown, 8 to 10 minutes. Add the raisins, sesame seeds, coriander seeds, cumin seeds, and oregano. Cook, stirring constantly, until the raisins are starting to soften and the spices are very fragrant, about 2 minutes. Add the chipotles with the adobo sauce and the vinegar and season generously with salt. Cook, stirring, until well combined, 1 minute.

4. Transfer the mixture to the food processor or blender with the tortilla and add the almond butter, chocolate-hazelnut spread, and ⅓ cup water. Process or blend the mixture until you have a smooth sauce. Taste it for

- 1½ teaspoons cumin seeds
- 1½ teaspoons dried oregano
- 1 to 3 canned chipotle chiles in adobo sauce (1 for a relatively mild sauce, 3 for a fairly spicy sauce), plus 1 tablespoon of the adobo sauce
- 1 tablespoon cider vinegar
- 2 heaping tablespoons almond butter
- 1 tablespoon plus 2 teaspoons chocolate-hazelnut spread, such as Nutella
- Crumbled *queso fresco* and pickled red onions (recipe follows), for serving

seasoning and add more salt or vinegar if you like. At this point, you can also add another 1 or 2 more chipotles, if you played it safe at first but now think you would like more heat. Refrigerate until about 20 minutes before you want to eat. Take the sauce out of the refrigerator at least 20 minutes before serving so that it can come to room temperature (or heat it in the microwave in 20-second bursts until just barely warm; you don't want it to cook).

5. Using tongs, lift the beef out of the slow cooker, leaving the fat and drippings behind, and place in a serving bowl or platter. Let the beef cool just enough to handle. Break up the beef into large, coarse pieces, using your hands or 2 forks. Pour the sauce over and toss to coat. Taste and season with salt if necessary. Serve the beef in the corn tortillas with *queso fresco* and pickled onion on top.

Good to know: You can make the sauce in the morning, when you put the beef in the slow cooker, or at night, right before you eat. Or you can make it up to two days ahead and store it in the refrigerator. I think that it tastes ever so slightly better if you make it ahead of time or in the morning so the flavors have a chance to deepen and mellow.

| ALL-DAY | Holds well on warm through step 1 for up to 2 hours | Prep time: 20 minutes | Slow-cook time: 8 to 10 hours |
| | | Finish time: 5 minutes | Equipment: 5- to 8-quart slow cooker |

Quick-Pickled Onions

I make these all the time and I don't usually measure the ingredients. You really can't mess them up. Thinly slice a small **red onion** and put it into a heatproof plastic container or nonreactive bowl. Bring about 1 cup of **vinegar** to a boil (I like cider vinegar but rice, white wine, or even regular white vinegar will work fine) in a nonreactive saucepan and stir in about

3 tablespoons **sugar** until dissolved (I tend to use granulated sugar, but you could also use honey or raw sugar) and a pinch of **salt**. Pour the boiling vinegar over the onions. The pickled onions are ready to use almost right away, as soon as they cool a bit, but they're best after an hour or so. The pickles keep in the refrigerator for at least a week.

Poultry

Orange, Olive, and Fennel
Chicken Tagine, 138

Orange, Olive, and Fennel Chicken Tagine

A tagine is a North African stew cooked in an earthenware pot of the same name, with a tall conical lid. Here, the slow cooker stands in for the tagine to make a warmly spiced chicken and vegetable braise.

1 tablespoon olive oil

4 large bone-in, skin-on chicken thighs (about 1½ pounds)

Kosher salt

1 large red or yellow onion, chopped

4 large garlic cloves, grated or finely minced

One 4-inch ginger knob, peeled and grated (about ¼ cup)

2 large or 3 to 4 small carrots (8 to 10 ounces total), sliced ½ inch thick

1 large fennel bulb and stalks, cored and sliced, fronds reserved for serving

1 teaspoon ground turmeric

1 teaspoon ground cumin

1 teaspoon ground coriander

1 teaspoon smoked paprika

½ teaspoon red pepper flakes

1. Warm the oil in a large skillet over high heat. Pat the chicken thighs dry and season them with salt on both sides. Carefully place the thighs in the hot oil skin side down and cook undisturbed, about 6 minutes, until the chicken skin is golden brown and crisp and some of the fat has rendered. At this point, the chicken thighs should release fairly easily from the pan—if they don't, let them cook a few minutes longer—but you might need to scrape under them with a spatula to get them up. Transfer the chicken, skin up, to a 5- to 8-quart slow cooker. Leave the drippings in the skillet.

2. Reduce the heat under the skillet to medium or medium-low if the chicken drippings look like they're starting to burn. Add the onion, season generously with salt, and cook, stirring occasionally, until softened, about 8 minutes. Add the garlic and ginger and cook, stirring, until fragrant and well combined, 1 minute. Add the carrots and fennel, season generously with salt, and cook, stirring, until the fennel just starts to soften, 2 minutes. Add the turmeric, cumin, coriander, paprika, red pepper flakes, and cinnamon and cook, stirring constantly, until all the ingredients are coated with the spices and the mixture is very fragrant, about 1 minute. Pour in the orange juice and wine, increase the heat to high, and cook until the liquid just starts to bubble, scraping up all the browned bits on the bottom of the pan with a spoon or spatula.

3. Pour the mixture into the slow cooker with the chicken and scatter the olives over the top. Cover and cook on LOW until the chicken and vegetables are tender, about 4 hours.

4. Slice off the tops and bottoms of the oranges so they sit flat on your cutting board. Following the curve of the fruit, cut off all the peel and bitter white pith from the oranges and discard. Your oranges are now naked.

- ½ teaspoon ground cinnamon
- ½ cup orange juice
- ¼ cup dry white wine
- ⅓ cup pitted, halved oil-cured olives
- 2 navel oranges
- Juice of ½ lemon
- Handful of chopped fresh flat-leaf parsley and couscous (about 1 cooked cup per person), for serving

Uncover the slow cooker. Holding the oranges over the slow cooker to catch the juice, cut between the membranes to release the segments into the tagine. Discard the membranes. (This is called "supreming" the orange, and the point of it is to have nice wedges of orange flesh without any chewy bits of membrane, pith, or peel. If you don't feel like doing it, you can also just peel the oranges and chop the segments into bite-size pieces, then add them to the pot.) Squeeze the lemon juice into the tagine and stir in the chopped parsley and reserved fennel fronds. Taste for seasoning and add more salt if necessary. Serve the tagine over cooked couscous.

Good to know: Any good-quality olive will work in this recipe, but I think oil-cured olives are worth seeking out. They're richer and less tart than most olives, meaty-textured, and almost metallic-flavored, in a strangely addictive way. I love the way they pair with sweet flavors, like the orange segments that finish this dish.

Holds well on warm through step 3 for up to 1 hour	Prep time: 30 minutes	Slow-cook time: 4 hours
	Finish time: 10 minutes	Equipment: 5- to 8-quart slow cooker

See the photo on page 137.

Turmeric Yogurt

The turmeric yogurt that's served with Harissa Pork Chili with Toppings Galore (page 176) is also delicious with this tagine. If you have time, just season 1 cup plain whole milk Greek yogurt with ¾ teaspoon turmeric and a generous pinch of salt. Stir until the turmeric is evenly distributed and the yogurt has turned a lovely pale yellow. Serve it on the side so people can dollop some on their bowls of tagine.

Gingery Chicken and Shiitake Congee

Congee is a Chinese rice porridge that's cooked low and slow until the rice is creamy and almost completely broken down. It's a dish that plays to the slow cooker's strengths. The finished congee is meant to be mild and comforting, an ideal dinner when you're tired or under the weather. It hinges on two things: the quality of the chicken broth, which should be the best you can make or lay your hands on, and the toppings, which liven up the congee to your liking. (I think it's best topped generously!)

1 pound boneless, skinless chicken thighs, cut into thirds

Kosher salt

3 quarts (12 cups) Classic Chicken Stock (page 5) or good-quality low-sodium chicken broth

1½ cups long-grain white rice, preferably jasmine

3 whole scallions, trimmed

8 ounces fresh shiitake mushrooms, stemmed and caps halved

3 garlic cloves, grated

One 3-inch ginger knob, peeled and grated (about 3 tablespoons), plus more for topping

Sliced trimmed scallions, for topping

Roasted salted peanuts, black vinegar, XO sauce, soy sauce, sesame oil, and/or chile oil, for topping

1. Season the chicken generously with salt. Combine the chicken, 1 to 2 more teaspoons salt (use 1 teaspoon if you're using salted store-bought broth; 2 teaspoons if you're using unsalted homemade broth), the stock, rice, whole scallions, mushrooms, garlic, and ginger in a 5- to 8-quart slow cooker and stir to combine. Cook on LOW until the rice is almost completely broken down, creamy, and glossy, about 6 hours.

2. Stir the congee and remove and discard the scallions. Season generously with salt to taste. Serve in bowls with freshly grated ginger and sliced scallions on top, plus the other toppings of your choice.

ALL-DAY	Holds (reasonably well) on warm through step 1 for up to 2 hours	Prep time: 15 minutes	Slow-cook time: 6 hours
		Finish time: 5 minutes	Equipment: 5- to 8-quart slow cooker

Green Pozole with Pumpkin Seeds, Chicken, and Collards

Cilantro, roasted poblanos, and tomatillos make this traditional Mexican stew tangy and herbal, while the pumpkin seeds add rustic texture and richness. I like the collards here, because they get tender and sweet but not mushy when slow-cooked.

6 garlic cloves

3 large poblano peppers, halved, stemmed, and seeded

2 jalapeños, stemmed and halved

1 large or medium white onion, quartered

1 bunch of fresh cilantro, including stems

1 pound tomatillos (about 8), husked, rinsed, and quartered

1 cup raw, hulled pumpkin seeds (pepitas)

Kosher salt

Three 15-ounce cans hominy, drained and rinsed

1 bunch of collard greens (about 10 ounces), stemmed and chopped

1 pound boneless, skinless chicken thighs

⅓ cup plain whole milk yogurt

Diced avocado, crumbled tortilla chips, and *queso fresco*, for topping

1. Preheat the broiler on high and position a rack 6 inches from the heat source (if that's how your broiler is configured). Spread out the garlic, poblanos, jalapeños, and onion on a rimmed baking sheet, placing the chiles skin side up. Broil on high for 5 to 10 minutes, until the vegetables are charred in spots and start to slump.

2. Put all the broiled vegetables into a blender and add the cilantro, tomatillos, pumpkin seeds, 1 tablespoon salt, and 5 cups water. If you can't fit all the ingredients in your blender, work in batches. Puree until smooth.

3. Pour the puree into a 5- to 8-quart slow cooker. Stir in the hominy, collard greens, and chicken, cover, and cook on LOW for 6 hours.

4. Open the lid and coarsely shred the chicken with two forks. Stir in the yogurt. Taste for seasoning and add more salt if necessary. Serve in bowls with the toppings.

Good to know: *If you, like me, are one of the unlucky people who find cilantro soapy, you'll be happy to know that pureeing magically deactivates the herb's unpleasant taste, leaving just the fresh, aromatic flavors behind.*

ALL-DAY	Holds well on warm through step 3 for up to 2 hours	Prep time: 20 minutes	Slow-cook time: 6 hours
		Finish time: 5 minutes	Equipment: 5- to 8-quart slow cooker

Miso-Butter Roast Chicken and Potatoes

MAKES 4 TO 6 SERVINGS

Slow-cooking a "roast" chicken yields moist, juicy meat but flabby skin—the easy fix is to run the carved chicken under the broiler to crisp the skin before serving. The miso-honey mixture that's drizzled on before broiling helps the skin get deep caramelization, and it also reinforces the salty-sweet miso flavor you added in the beginning, which will have mellowed. You can serve this as a full meal on its own or add a side dish of spinach sautéed with a little ginger.

4 tablespoons (½ stick) unsalted butter, at room temperature

¾ cup white or yellow miso paste

1½ pounds small new potatoes, halved

One 4- to 5-pound chicken

¼ cup honey

1 small bunch of chives, thinly sliced, for topping

Lemon wedges, for serving

1. Preheat an empty 5- to 8-quart slow cooker on **HIGH** for 10 to 15 minutes while you're getting everything ready. Combine the butter and ½ cup of the miso in a medium bowl and mash them together to make a uniform mixture. Put the potatoes into the bottom of the slow cooker and add a small dollop of the miso butter; stir to coat. Season the potatoes lightly with salt. Pat the chicken dry and rub the remaining butter all over the chicken, and especially under the skin of the breasts directly on the breast meat: To do this, gently loosen the skin and separate it from the breast meat by sliding your fingers under the skin, then tuck some butter in there. Set the chicken on top of the potatoes.

2. Cover the slow cooker and reduce the heat to **LOW**. Cook for 5 to 6 hours (the larger the slow cooker, the shorter the cook time), until the chicken breast registers 160°F internal temperature on an instant-read or probe thermometer when you check the top of the breast. Also check that the thickest part of the thigh and the juice in the cavity register at least 165°F. Cooking the chicken much beyond these temperatures will result in dry meat, so this is a case when pulling out the thermometer really makes a difference.

3. Turn off and uncover the slow cooker and let the chicken rest for 10 minutes. Meanwhile, preheat the broiler on high and position a rack 6 inches from the heat source (if that's how your broiler works). Line a baking sheet with foil or parchment paper. In a small bowl mix together the honey and remaining ¼ cup miso.

4. Using tongs slung through the cavity of the chicken and your hands to support it, carefully transfer the chicken from the slow cooker to a cutting board, leaving the drippings behind. Remove the potatoes from the slow cooker with a slotted spoon and put them on the prepared baking

sheet. Carve the chicken and put the pieces on the baking sheet skin side up. Drizzle the chicken all over with the miso-honey mixture, then broil the potatoes and chicken until the chicken skin is caramelized and crisp, dark golden brown, about 5 minutes. (Don't walk away; the skin will burn quickly because of the sugar in the honey.)

5. Put the chicken pieces and potatoes on a serving platter (or leave them on the baking sheet and serve them straight from that) and drizzle a little juice from the slow cooker over the whole thing. Top with chives and serve with lemon wedges.

Holds on warm through step 2 for up to 30 minutes	Prep time: 10 minutes	Slow-cook time: 5 to 6 hours
	Finish time: 20 minutes	Equipment: 5- to 8-quart slow cooker

Luxury Chicken Breasts with Herb Aioli

MAKES 4 SERVINGS

Very slow, gentle poaching in herb-infused olive oil turns chicken breasts extremely juicy and flavorful, with a firm but velvety texture. You then use the herbed poaching oil to make a quick creamy aioli and serve it with the chicken. It's as lush and over the top as chicken breast can possibly get.

This recipe has several steps, but they're all very easy and hands-off. You can also poach the chicken and make the aioli ahead of time and serve it chilled.

¼ cup fine table salt

¼ cup sugar

1 lemon, quartered

4 boneless, skinless chicken breast halves (about 2 pounds)

3 cups extra-virgin olive oil

3 garlic cloves

2 bay leaves

2 thyme sprigs

1 rosemary sprig

1 teaspoon black peppercorns

2 large egg yolks

½ teaspoon kosher salt

Juice of ½ lemon

Green salad and bread, for serving

1. In a large bowl or gallon-size zip-top bag, combine 5 cups cold water with the table salt, sugar, and 2 of the lemon quarters. Stir to dissolve the salt and sugar, then add the chicken. Seal the container or bag and refrigerate for at least 1 hour and up to 8 hours.

2. Meanwhile, in a 4- to 6-quart slow cooker, combine the oil, garlic, bay leaves, thyme and rosemary sprigs, peppercorns, and the remaining 2 lemon quarters. Cover and cook on LOW until the oil registers 200°F on an instant-read thermometer, about 1 hour. If you want to let the oil infuse more deeply, or if you want to start the recipe in the morning and finish it later, set the oil to cook on LOW for 1 hour and let it switch to WARM for up to 7 hours. Increase the heat to low and bring the oil back up to 200°F before proceeding.

3. Pull the chicken from the brine with tongs, pat it dry with a paper towel, and carefully place it in the oil. (Discard the brine.) Cook for about 40 minutes on LOW, until the thickest part of the chicken registers 155°F on a probe or instant-read thermometer. (It's very important to cook to temperature for this dish because if the chicken overcooks at all, it won't be nearly as lush and velvety. The very easiest way to do this is to use a probe thermometer: Just stick it in the thickest part of one chicken breast, close the lid, and set the thermometer to alarm when it hits 155°F.)

4. Using tongs, remove the chicken, lemon, herbs, and garlic cloves from the oil and set the chicken on a cutting board to rest, tented with foil. You need one of the cooked garlic cloves for the aioli. You can save the other aromatics for garnish or discard them.

5. Ladle out 1 cup of the infused oil, carefully tipping the insert to get oil without peppercorns in it. Let the oil cool slightly until you can put your finger in it comfortably, about 10 minutes.

6. To make the aioli, in a small bowl or large liquid measuring cup combine the egg yolks, kosher salt, the lemon juice, and the reserved cooked garlic clove. Use an immersion blender to blend the mixture until light and a little frothy, about 1 minute. (If you don't have an immersion blender you can also make the aioli in a regular blender using the same process.) Add the cooled oil a tablespoon at a time, making sure each tablespoon of oil is incorporated before adding more. Go slowly, though at the end the aioli will be more stable and you can add the oil a little faster. Repeat until all the oil is incorporated and you have a lovely, thick aioli.

7. Slice the chicken thickly, crosswise against the grain. Serve the chicken with the aioli and a green salad and good bread on the side.

Good to know: Strain the leftover infused oil and refrigerate it in a sealed container. Use it within 1 week to sauté chicken or vegetables, make chicken soup, or fry eggs.

ALL-DAY	Holds well on warm through step 2 for up to 7 hours	Prep time: 1 hour 10 minutes (includes infusing the poaching oil in the slow cooker)	Slow-cook time: 40 minutes
		Finish time: 15 minutes	Equipment: 4- to 6-quart slow cooker

Buttery Duck Confit

MAKES 4 SERVINGS

Instead of cooking the duck legs in duck fat, as you would for a traditional confit, here you confit in butter, which is cheaper, easier to find, and just as delicious. I've adapted the idea from the blog Alexandra's Kitchen. *There is no way to mess this up: The duck legs just slowly bubble away in their own fat and the melted butter. (Don't worry, you're not going to end up eating all that fat, as very little is absorbed into the meat—the buttery flavor, though, is abundant.) The result is silky, rich meat and, once you sear it, crackly skin. It's incredibly delicious, and just as good as the more labor-intensive original. If you do happen to have duck fat on hand, feel free to substitute it for some or all of the butter.*

4 duck legs (about 2 pounds, but this recipe will work with any size legs)

Kosher salt and freshly ground black pepper

½ pound (2 sticks) unsalted butter, melted

3 thyme sprigs

3 garlic cloves, halved

Green salad and bread, for serving

1. Optional (but recommended) dry brine: Put the duck legs into a sealable container, pat them dry, and rub them all over with 1 tablespoon kosher salt and lots of pepper. Refrigerate overnight.

2. Set the duck legs in a 5- to 8-quart slow cooker—no need to pat them dry again or remove the brine, and it's fine if they overlap. If you haven't done the overnight dry brine, pat the legs dry and season them generously on all sides with salt and pepper. Pour the melted butter over the top and add the thyme and garlic. Cover and cook for 8 hours on LOW.

3. Pull the duck legs out of the fat with tongs. (Strain the thyme and garlic from the fat and discard them, then pour the fat into a container, refrigerate it for up to 2 weeks, and keep it for other uses, like roasting potatoes.) Put the duck legs skin side down into a dry skillet over medium-high heat. Crisp the legs on both sides, about 4 minutes per side. Serve them with your favorite salad and a hunk of bread, or use them in Duck Confit, Escarole, and Fennel Salad with Clementines (page 150) or The DLT (page 152).

Good to know: If you're not going to eat the duck legs right away, you can store them like a traditional confit, covered in their fat in the fridge. Simply put the duck into a container and pour the fat over the top, making sure that all the duck is covered by fat. Cover the container and store in the refrigerator for up to 2 weeks. Then just pull the legs out of the fat and crisp them in a skillet before eating, as described in step 3.

ALL-DAY	Holds well on warm through step 2 for up to 3 hours	Prep time: 5 minutes plus optional overnight brine	Slow-cook time: 8 hours
		Finish time: 15 minutes	Equipment: 5- to 8-quart slow cooker

Duck Confit, Escarole, and Fennel Salad with Clementines

MAKES 4 SERVINGS

This is a great way to serve duck confit when you want something a little light and bright—winter salad at its best. The sharp and citrusy ingredients balance the duck's richness beautifully.

Buttery Duck Confit (page 149) or 4 store-bought confit duck legs

4 clementines

1 escarole head, torn into large pieces

1 small fennel bulb, cored and very thinly sliced, preferably on a mandoline, a few fronds reserved for topping

1 small shallot, minced

3 tablespoons white wine vinegar

1 tablespoon orange juice

2 teaspoons Dijon mustard

2 teaspoons honey

Kosher salt

⅓ cup extra-virgin olive oil

½ bunch of chives, thinly sliced, for topping

1. Scoop the duck confit out of its fat if it has been stored in the fridge. (If you've just made it, simply proceed from here.) Put the duck legs skin side down into a dry skillet over medium-high heat. Crisp the legs on both sides, about 4 minutes per side. Remove from the heat and set aside.

2. Zest 1 clementine into a large liquid measuring cup, then peel all 4 clementines and thinly slice them crosswise (through the equator). In a serving bowl, combine the sliced clementines, escarole, and fennel.

3. Add the shallot, vinegar, orange juice, mustard, honey, and 1 teaspoon salt to the measuring cup with the zest and whisk to combine. Whisk in the oil.

4. Drizzle the dressing over the salad sparingly and toss to coat the salad evenly. Coarsely shred the duck meat and the crisp skin and add it to the salad. (Discard the bones.) Toss again. Taste and add more salt and/or more dressing if necessary. Top with the chives and reserved fennel fronds.

Total time: 30 minutes

The DLT
(aka Duck, Lettuce, and Tomato; aka the Most Delicious Sandwich in the World)

MAKES 4 SANDWICHES

Scoop 4 legs **Buttery Duck Confit** (page 149) out of the fat if they have been stored in the fridge. (If you've just made the confit, simply proceed from here.) Put the duck legs skin side down into a dry skillet over medium-high heat. Crisp the legs on both sides, about 4 minutes per side. Set aside to let cool a bit. Meanwhile, toast 8 slices of **good white bread** and spread them with **mayonnaise**. On the 4 bottom slices of bread, layer thick slices of ripe, in-season **tomato** and then season with **salt**. Add **green- or red-leaf lettuce**. Coarsely shred the duck meat and skin and discard the bones. Pile a serving of duck on each of the sandwiches and top each with the second piece of bread (you may have some duck left over).

Total time: 15 minutes

Corn, Mushroom,
and Zucchini Tamales

Parties

I have a theory about dinner parties: The key to a good one (i.e., one you actually enjoy) is taking a shower after the cooking is done and before your friends arrive—it's a reset button. The recipes in this chapter are more involved than the dishes in the other chapters in this book, but they allow you some breathing room before dinner. Most of the effort happens well before serving, so there's no running around the kitchen at the last minute.

All-day recipes: These recipes can cook or hold on warm unattended for 8 hours or more.

Having Friends over for Dinner

I'm not good at entertaining—I don't own more than four plates that match, I serve wine in jelly jars (not because they're twee but because they're what I have), and there are usually LEGOs on the floor. But having friends over for dinner is absolutely, hands down, my favorite way to spend an evening. My favorite people, with their feet up on my couch, getting loud about politics—to me, it's better than any bar or restaurant (and I don't have to pay for a babysitter). I think a lot of people deny themselves this pleasure because they feel pressure to "entertain," which means that everything—music, dishes, food—needs to be curated and perfect. Blame Instagram and Facebook, or blame Martha Stewart, but trust me: If you invite people into your home, give them a glass of wine, and feed them something tasty and warm, they're going to have a good time. No one cares that the plates don't match. No one is looking at the ball of cat hair under the couch, and if they are, refill their wineglass. You're not entertaining—you're just having some friends over for dinner! Here are seven pointers to keep in mind:

1. Have one bottle of wine on hand per guest who drinks alcohol. It's unlikely you'll go through that much, but running out of wine at a dinner party is tragic. It's better to have extra.

2. If there will be guests who don't drink alcohol, make sure you have something special to offer them, too. Fever-Tree makes wonderful tonics, ginger ale, and bitter lemon soda. Fentimans makes really fun and delicious old-fashioned sodas. If there's nothing like that at your supermarket, plain sparkling water with a splash of cranberry or pomegranate juice is nice.

3. Set out something to snack on for when your friends arrive. I know it seems obvious, but it really takes the pressure off you: If dinner's late for whatever reason, no one gets too hungry or too tipsy. And there's no need to overthink it. You could keep it as simple as nice supermarket cheddar, crackers, and apple slices.

4. Take a quick shower before everyone comes. (Even if it means there are LEGOs all over the floor. It's more important.)

5. Plan to have too much food. You want to have leftovers—if everything is gone, I always feel that someone might not have gotten to eat as much as they would have liked.

6. You can make dessert in the slow cooker (the timing on, say, the Sticky Toffee Pudding with Maple Caramel on page 188 is perfect for putting in just before people arrive and serving after dinner), but if you want to avoid making dessert altogether, no one has ever objected to a couple of cartons of really good ice cream. Talenti gelato is available widely now, and it is outrageously good.

7. Don't do the dishes until everyone's gone home (unless you're trying to get people to go home). Pile them in the sink and deal with them later.

Spring Vegetable Risotto
with Parmesan Broth, 158

Spring Vegetable Risotto with Parmesan Broth

MAKES 4 TO 6 SERVINGS

This creamy risotto is a simple, delicate way to showcase the flavors of spring; homemade stock and fresh spring asparagus are key. Adding a beautiful topping makes it special: The simplest option is a flurry of sliced radishes and herbs, but you can really fancy it up with edible flowers (like pansies, hibiscus, or violets) or flowering pea shoots, which are at farmers' markets in the spring.

3 tablespoons unsalted butter

2 large or 3 medium-small leeks, white and light green parts only, thinly sliced (about 4 cups)

Kosher salt

6½ cups Parmesan-Garlic Broth (page 4) or Classic Chicken Stock (page 5)

2 cups Arborio rice

½ cup dry white wine

Freshly ground black pepper

1 pound asparagus, trimmed and cut into 1-inch pieces

1½ cups fresh or frozen peas

1. Melt the butter in a large skillet over medium-high heat. Add the leeks, season generously with 2 big pinches of salt, and cook, stirring often, until softened and wilted, about 10 minutes.

2. Meanwhile, bring 4 cups of the Parmesan-Garlic Broth to a boil in a small saucepan.

3. Add the rice to the skillet with the leeks, season with salt, and cook, stirring, until the rice starts to turn translucent, about 4 minutes. Add the wine, stir, and let it be absorbed by the rice, which happens almost immediately. Season generously with black pepper.

4. Combine the boiling broth and the leek-rice mixture in a 5- to 7-quart slow cooker. Season with ½ teaspoon salt and stir well to combine. Cover and cook on HIGH until the rice is nearly tender and has absorbed most of the stock, about 1 hour. Stir in the asparagus, cover, and cook until the asparagus is crisp-tender, 10 to 15 more minutes.

5. Meanwhile, bring the remaining 2½ cups of broth to a boil in a medium saucepan and add the peas. Frozen peas will be done almost immediately, but fresh peas will need to simmer until tender, about 5 minutes. When the asparagus is done, pour the broth and the peas into the slow

1½ cups finely grated Parmesan, plus more for serving

Juice of 1 lemon

Edible flowers, pea shoots, very thinly sliced radishes, sliced scallions, and/or chopped fresh tarragon, for topping

cooker (the risotto needs more liquid than it seems to) and stir well for a minute. The rice will slowly soak up the additional liquid. Add the Parmesan and lemon juice and season generously with black pepper. Taste and adjust the seasoning if you like. Serve immediately, topped with flowers, scallions, radishes, and/or tarragon. Pass a little bowl of more Parmesan at the table.

Good to know: When buying asparagus, choosing thick or thin spears is just a matter of preference; both are equally good. But make sure the bottom stem ends are moist and supple (not dried out or cracked) and the top tips are plump and tightly furled.

| Does not hold well on warm | Prep time: 20 minutes | Slow-cook time: About 1 hour 15 minutes |
| | Finish time: 15 minutes | Equipment: 5- to 7-quart slow cooker |

See the photo on page 157.

Corn, Mushroom, and Zucchini Tamales

MAKES ABOUT 12 TAMALES, 6 TO 12 APPETIZER OR 4 MAIN COURSE SERVINGS

Traditionally, tamale dough is usually made with lard, but I think it's relatively difficult to find good lard—not the hydrogenated stuff in the supermarket—while very easy to find good butter. I wondered if a buttery tamale dough would taste good, and of course it does! Especially with this delicate three-vegetable filling, which is best made in summer but can be enjoyed year-round with frozen corn.

FILLING

3 tablespoons unsalted butter

3 garlic cloves, grated or minced

1 medium to large zucchini (about 8 ounces), cut into ½-inch dice (about 2 cups)

8 ounces cremini mushrooms, stemmed and finely chopped

Kosher salt

Kernels from 1 plump ear corn or ¾ cup frozen corn

2 scallions, white and light green parts only, trimmed and thinly sliced

1 teaspoon cumin seeds

1 teaspoon dried oregano

1 teaspoon red pepper flakes

¼ cup jarred tomatillo salsa

1 cup grated *cotija* cheese

1. Make the filling: Melt the butter in a large skillet over medium-high heat. Add the garlic and cook for 1 minute, stirring, until fragrant. Add the zucchini and mushrooms, season generously with salt, and cook, stirring occasionally, until their moisture has evaporated and they have started to brown, about 10 minutes. Add the corn and scallions and stir to combine. Cook for 1 minute. Add the cumin, oregano, and red pepper flakes and cook, stirring, until fragrant, 1 minute. Remove from the heat and stir in the salsa. Taste and add salt if necessary—the filling should be delicious on its own. The filling can be made up to 2 days ahead; keep it refrigerated in an airtight container.

2. Soak the corn husks: Put about 18 corn husks into either a plugged sink (the easiest option) or a very large bowl. Cover the husks with water and weigh them down with small plates or bowls to make sure they are all submerged. (You have extra husks to make ties and also in case some rip.) Let them soak while you make the tamale dough.

3. Make the dough: In a stand mixer fitted with the paddle attachment, beat the butter on medium-high speed until it is lightened in color, creamy, and fluffy, 3 to 5 minutes. Meanwhile, in a medium bowl, stir together the tamale flour, hot water, oil, salt, and baking powder. Mix it with your hands just until it comes together into a uniform dough. With the stand mixer still running, add the dough to the butter in small handfuls, letting each handful get incorporated before adding more and stopping to scrape down the sides of the bowl at least twice, until all the dough is incorporated into the butter. Continue to beat the dough on medium-high until it is extremely fluffy, almost like frosting, about 10 minutes. (You can do this with a handheld mixer, but it takes closer to 15 minutes and is very tiring.) You're done when a small bit of dough floats when you drop it into a glass of water.

DOUGH

½ pound (2 sticks) unsalted butter, at room temperature, cut into small bits

3 cups tamale flour (labeled "tamal" or "masa mix for tamales")

2 cups hot tap water

½ cup canola oil

2 teaspoons kosher salt

1 teaspoon baking powder

SERVING

Salsas, for topping

Heirloom tomatoes, thickly sliced and salted (optional)

4. Put a rack in the bottom of a 6- to 8-quart slow cooker. If you don't have a rack that fits, roll and crumple two 2-foot-long sheets of foil into 2 snakes. Use the foil to make 2 coils in the bottom of the slow cooker, so that the tamales will have a spot to sit. Now pour water into the slow cooker to a depth of about 1 inch, just below the rack or foil.

5. Drain the corn husks. Pick a large husk, and working with the natural grain of the husk, rip off about 12 thin strips that you can use as ties. (If necessary, you can use more than 1 husk to make ties; that's why you have extras.)

6. Assemble the tamales: Working with 1 husk at a time, position the husk so that the more pointed end is facing you (closest to your stomach) and the wider end is away from you. Spread a heaping ¼ cup dough into the center of the husk and then put a heaping 2 tablespoons of filling in a strip down the center of the dough. Sprinkle about 1 tablespoon of cheese on the filling. Fold the 2 sides up (almost like you're closing a book) so that the dough meets in the middle to enclose the filling inside, then pull 1 side of the husk over the other. Fold the bottom of the husk up to close the package, leaving just the top open. Secure the husk with one of the strips tied around the middle. (See How to Assemble the Tamales on pages 162–163.) Place the tamale on its side in the slow cooker. (Don't worry, the filling will not spill out.) Repeat with the remaining dough to make about 12 tamales, piling the tamales on top of each other to fill the insert. (If you have extra filling, it makes excellent tacos.)

7. Cover and cook on **HIGH** for 3 to 4 hours, until the dough is firm and pulls away from the husk when you check it. (Eight-quart cookers will generally cook faster, closer to the 3-hour mark, while 6-quart cookers will take a little longer.)

8. Set the tamales on a serving platter. Serve them with your favorite salsas on the side and, if you want, with heirloom tomato slices, to make it a full meal.

Good to know: Technically, these tamales aren't vegetarian because cotija cheese, like many cheeses, is usually made with rennet, an animal product. So if you have strict vegetarians coming to dinner, use a cheese that's labeled as vegetarian. You can also leave the cheese out entirely, though that's not as much fun.

Holds well on warm through step 7 for up to 30 minutes	Prep time: 1 hour	Slow-cook time: 3 to 4 hours	Equipment: 6- to 8-quart slow cooker and about 18 dried corn husks

See the photo on page 154.

How to Assemble the Tamales

1. Spread a corn husk with a heaping ¼ cup dough, then top it with a heaping 2 tablespoons filling in a line down the middle of the dough. Sprinkle the filling with about 1 tablespoon cheese.

2. Hold the husk by its sides and fold the sides up to meet at the top . . .

5. Now open the sides back up and pull one side of the husk over the tamale . . .

6. . . . followed by the other, to close the tamale into a roll.

3. . . . almost like you're closing a book. Press the dough together at the top.

4. The dough will stick together to enclose the filling.

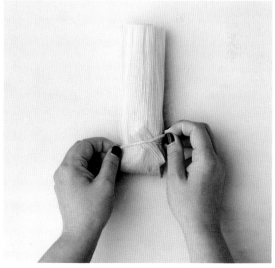

7. Fold the bottom end of the husk up, leaving only the top open.

8. And finally, tie the tamale closed with a torn strip of husk.

Proper Red Sauce Eggplant Parm

A great eggplant Parm depends on the contrast between the olive-oiled crispness of the eggplant breading and the softness of everything else: cheese, sauce, creamy eggplant insides. So every now and again, especially on cold days, it's nice to relax into the work of slicing, salting, dipping, and frying eggplant. After that, the work's done. It's just a matter of having your favorite red sauce on hand (either store-bought or homemade) and layering it all together with cheese and herbs in the slow cooker.

In New England, where I grew up, eggplant Parm is always served with a side of pasta. You can absolutely do that—linguine is a good choice—but I feel that the eggplant is enough on its own, especially with some good bread and a big glass of wine.

2 pounds Italian eggplant (about 2 large eggplants), sliced into ½-inch-thick rounds

Kosher salt

4 large eggs

3 cups panko bread crumbs (see note, opposite)

1 teaspoon red pepper flakes

2 garlic cloves, minced or grated

Olive oil, for shallow frying

3½ cups tomato sauce, such as 1 recipe Winter Tomato Sauce (page 8) or one 24-ounce jar of your favorite store-bought tomato sauce

1. Spread the eggplant slices out on paper towels and sprinkle them generously with salt. Flip and repeat. Let the eggplant sit for 1 hour.

2. Beat the eggs in a medium shallow bowl with a pinch of salt. Combine the bread crumbs, red pepper flakes, garlic, and 2 teaspoons salt in a large shallow bowl. Pour enough oil into a large skillet to generously cover the bottom of the pan.

3. Blot the eggplant dry. Warm the oil over medium-high heat. Dip an eggplant slice first in the egg and then in the bread crumbs, pressing and dredging with your hands to get a good bread-crumb coating on each slice. Carefully lay the eggplant into the pan and then repeat to fill the pan with 1 layer of eggplant. (You're going to fry in batches to avoid crowding the pan.) Cook until deeply golden on the bottom, 3 to 4 minutes, then flip and repeat, 3 to 4 minutes. Lay the fried eggplant on paper towels to drain. Repeat with the remaining eggplant to fry all the slices in about 4 batches total, replenishing the oil as needed and wiping out the pan with a paper towel if the bread-crumb residue starts to burn.

4. Pour about ½ cup tomato sauce into a 5- to 8-quart slow cooker, just to coat the bottom. Lay about one-third of the eggplant slices down in an even layer on top. Scatter about one-third of the parsley and one-third of the Parmesan over the eggplant. Spoon half of the remaining tomato sauce over the top. Repeat once (eggplant-parsley-Parmesan-sauce) and then finish with a last layer of the remaining eggplant, parsley, and Parmesan on top.

½ cup finely chopped fresh flat-leaf parsley, plus more for serving

1 cup finely grated Parmesan, plus more for serving

8 ounces fresh mozzarella, thinly sliced

Sliced fresh basil, for serving

5. Place a double layer of paper towels over the top of the cooker to soak up condensation, leaving some overhang so that the paper towels don't fall onto the eggplant, and then close the lid on top of the paper towels (see page xx for a how-to). Cook on LOW for about 4 hours. If you put your ear next to the cooker, you'll hear the dish bubbling when it's just about done.

6. Uncover the cooker and layer the sliced fresh mozzarella on top of the eggplant. Close the lid and cook on LOW until the cheese is melted, about 10 minutes. Turn off the slow cooker, uncover, and let the eggplant rest for at least 10 minutes before serving. Serve straight from the insert and pass more parsley and Parmesan and the basil at the table.

Good to know:

* Many people salt eggplant to remove bitterness. I have never felt eggplant is particularly bitter, but here, the salting step is essential to remove excess moisture, which is not the slow cooker's friend.

* You must use panko—extra-coarse, extra-crisp Japanese-style bread crumbs—for the breading or the crunch will not survive the slow cooking.

Holds on warm through step 5 for up to 1 hour	Prep time: 1 hour 40 minutes (1 hour of this is inactive)	Slow-cook time: 4 hours
	Finish time: 20 minutes	Equipment: 5- to 8-quart slow cooker

Banana Leaf-Ancho Chile Lamb Tacos

MAKES 6 TO 8 SERVINGS

This recipe was inspired by barbacoa, *a Latin American and Caribbean term for flavorful, rich meat—often lamb, goat, or cow's head—that's wrapped in leaves and steamed in a pit. Here, the slow cooker plays the part of the pit and the banana leaves impart an aromatic, sweet flavor to the chile-rubbed lamb. Of course, you can also make the lamb without the banana leaves—just put the lamb and the marinade directly into your slow cooker.*

    I think this recipe works best with lamb shoulder, which gets supertender and lush when braised, but leg of lamb works very well also. If you don't want to use lamb at all, you can substitute the same quantity of beef chuck, which is sometimes more affordable and easier to find than lamb. Or, if you can get your hands on some goat, that would be even better.

6 dried ancho chiles

1 large white onion, quartered

5 large unpeeled garlic cloves

2 teaspoons red pepper flakes

2 teaspoons dried oregano

1½ teaspoons cumin seeds

Kosher salt

2 banana leaves, plus more for serving (optional; see note, page 168)

One 3- to 4-pound boneless lamb shoulder or leg

2 tablespoons canola oil

Corn tortillas (about 2 per person), lime wedges, salsas, and hot sauce, for serving

1. Warm a large skillet over medium-high heat. Add the chiles, onion, and garlic cloves to the dry skillet and let the ingredients toast, turning occasionally, until they are fragrant, 5 to 6 minutes. (Do this in batches if your skillet isn't big enough.) The chiles are done when they lighten slightly in color, puff up a little, and become pliable. The garlic and onion are done when they soften slightly and start to brown in spots. Put the chiles into a medium bowl and cover them with hot water. Peel the garlic. Put the garlic and onion into a blender with the red pepper flakes, oregano, and cumin. Add 1 teaspoon salt and ½ cup water. Set aside the blender and the chiles. Leave the skillet on the stove.

2. Optional: If you have a gas stove, turn a burner to medium-high heat. Holding a banana leaf at each end, slowly run it along the flame once or twice (don't worry, it will not catch on fire). Repeat with the other banana leaf. This step is not totally necessary, but it wakes the leaves up and makes them more fragrant.

3. Put 1 banana leaf into a 6- to 8-quart slow cooker, with the ends hanging out of the cooker on either side. Set the other leaf aside.

4. Pat the lamb dry and season it generously all over with salt. Warm the oil over high heat in the large skillet. Add the lamb and sear on all sides until deep brown, about 5 minutes per side. Put the lamb into the slow cooker, on top of the banana leaf.

5. Drain the chiles and stem them. (You can leave the seeds in.) Tear the chiles into pieces and put them into the blender with the other ingredients. Puree into a sauce. Pour the sauce all over the lamb, turning the meat to evenly coat it. Wrap the 2 dangling ends of the banana leaf over the lamb. Place the second leaf on top of the lamb, nestling it underneath so that the lamb is surrounded by the leaves. Cover and cook on LOW until the lamb is very tender, about 7 hours.

6. Transfer the meat to a large bowl, shred it, and toss it with the sauce. Discard the leaves. Use fresh banana leaves to cover a serving platter, if you like. Put the meat on the platter and serve with warmed tortillas, lime wedges, salsas, and hot sauce.

Good to know: You can order frozen banana leaves from Temple of Thai (templeofthai.com) or find them fresh or frozen at a market that carries Latin American or Caribbean products. If you buy frozen, just defrost them in the fridge first.

| ALL-DAY | Holds well on warm through step 5 for up to 2 hours | Prep time: 35 minutes | Slow-cook time: 7 hours |
| | | Finish time: 5 minutes | Equipment: 6- to 8-quart slow cooker |

Oxtail and Short Rib Pho

Pho is a Vietnamese rice noodle soup that's made in different ways in different regions but is generally characterized by a wonderfully aromatic broth. It is not traditional to make pho in the slow cooker, of course, but this streamlined technique works really well. You start with nothing more than water, aromatics, and bony cuts of beef, and the pho makes its own broth as it cooks. The key is using collagen-rich, bone-in cuts such as short ribs and oxtail, which will yield both a rich broth and tender meat after braising. The broiling step in the beginning ensures that the broth isn't too fatty.

2 pounds oxtail, cut into rounds (this is normally how oxtail is sold)

1½ pounds bone-in English-cut beef short ribs

One 4-inch ginger knob, peeled and halved lengthwise

3 large scallions, trimmed

Kosher salt

5 whole star anise

1 cinnamon stick

1 teaspoon whole cloves

1 teaspoon black peppercorns

1. Preheat the broiler on high and position a rack 6 inches below the heat source (if that's how your broiler works). Line a baking sheet with parchment or foil. Arrange the oxtail, short ribs, ginger, and scallions in a single layer on the prepared baking sheet. Pat the meat dry and season everything generously with salt. Now you'll broil these ingredients in order to get nice browning on the aromatics and meat, and also render out a lot of the meat's fat. Put the baking sheet under the broiler for 5 to 6 minutes, then check the scallions and pull them out if they're already nicely browned or charred in spots. Flip the meat. Put the baking sheet back under the broiler for another 5 to 10 minutes, until the meat is very deeply browned and the ginger is lightly toasted or charred in spots.

2. Using tongs, put the meat into the bottom of a 6- to 8-quart slow cooker (leave the fat behind on the sheet pan and discard it), then nestle the scallions and ginger around it. Top with the star anise, cinnamon, cloves, black peppercorns, fennel seeds, and 1 tablespoon salt. Add 8 cups cold water. Cover and cook on LOW for 8 hours.

3. Cook the noodles according to the package directions, then drain and rinse them in warm water.

½ teaspoon fennel seeds

1 pound 8 ounces (one and a half 16-ounce boxes) flat rice noodles

1 tablespoon fish sauce

1 tablespoon packed light brown sugar or raw demerara sugar

Lime wedges, basil and mint leaves, bean sprouts, thinly sliced jalapeños, and/or sliced scallions, for topping

Hoisin sauce and sriracha sauce, for serving (optional)

4. Remove the slow cooker lid. With a ladle, skim off any solids or foam from the surface of the soup, as well as any obvious fat. With tongs, pull out the oxtail and short ribs and put them into a large bowl. Stir the fish sauce and sugar into the broth and then strain the broth through a fine-mesh strainer into a second large bowl. Let the meat and broth cool very slightly, about 3 minutes. Shred the meat and discard the bones. Season the shredded meat with salt if it tastes flat. Ladle the layer of fat from the top of the broth and discard it, then taste the broth and season it if necessary with salt, fish sauce, and/or sugar. It should taste very balanced and heady with spices.

5. Layer servings of cooked noodles and handfuls of meat into large individual serving bowls. Pour the hot broth over the top. Serve with lime wedges, basil and mint, bean sprouts, jalapeños, and/or scallions on top. Pass hoisin and sriracha sauces at the table.

ALL-DAY	Holds well on warm through step 2 for up to 2 hours	Prep time: 20 minutes	Slow-cook time: 8 hours
		Finish time: 20 minutes	Equipment: 6- to 8-quart slow cooker

Cilantro, Mint, and Green Chile Lamb Biryani

MAKES 6 TO 8 SERVINGS

This recipe's technique is adapted from Neela Paniz's wonderful book The New Indian Slow Cooker. *The vibrant flavor of the herb and spice masala is inspired by my mother-in-law and my husband, who are the best cooks I know, and whose Maharashtrian food often showcases lots of herbs and green chiles. Biryani is rich and filling, so the striking freshness of the masala is key to balancing the dish as a whole.*

Biryani is traditionally cooked in a covered container, often sealed with a simple dough that's cracked open at the table for a dramatic show of aromatic steam. It turns out that the slow cooker can do almost exactly the same kind of thing, sealed with a sheet of foil. This dish is a project that takes about an hour of work to put together. But after that, it cooks completely unattended (don't peek), and there's nothing else to do except bring it to the table when it's done, a one-pot feast.

RICE

2 cups basmati rice

4 green cardamom pods

2 cinnamon sticks

MASALA AND LAMB

2 tablespoons unsalted butter

1 large yellow or red onion, roughly chopped

Kosher salt

5 garlic cloves, chopped

2 jalapeños or other green chiles, 1 seeded, both chopped

One 1-inch ginger knob, peeled and chopped (about 1 tablespoon)

2 teaspoons ground coriander

1. Soak the rice: Rinse the rice in a fine-mesh strainer until the water runs clear. Put the rice into a medium bowl and cover it with cool water. Soak for 20 minutes.

2. Make the masala: Melt the butter in a large skillet over medium-high heat. Add the onion, season generously with salt, and cook, stirring often, until softened and starting to brown, about 8 minutes. Add the garlic and jalapeños and cook, stirring often, until softened, 3 minutes. Stir in the fresh ginger, coriander, cardamom, cloves, cumin, turmeric, and ground ginger and cook until fragrant and combined, about 30 seconds. Add 1 tablespoon water and stir, scraping the bottom of the pan. Scrape the mixture into a blender and set aside to cool slightly. Leave the skillet on the stove. (No need to clean it.)

3. Make the rice: Put the cardamom pods and cinnamon sticks into a medium saucepan along with 6 cups well-salted water and bring it to a boil. Drain the rice through a fine-mesh strainer and add it to the pot. When the water comes back to a boil, give it a stir and cook, uncovered, about 3 more minutes, or until about halfway cooked—chewable but still noticeably crunchy in the middle. Drain the rice back into the fine-mesh strainer and run cold water over it to stop the cooking. Spread it evenly

½ teaspoon ground
  cardamom

½ teaspoon ground
  cloves

½ teaspoon ground
  cumin

½ teaspoon ground
  turmeric

¼ teaspoon ground
  ginger

1 tablespoon canola oil

3 pounds boneless
  lamb shoulder or leg,
  trimmed of excess fat
  and cut into 2-inch
  chunks

2 large bunches of
  fresh cilantro, leaves
  and stems roughly
  chopped

1 packed cup fresh
  mint leaves (from
  about ½ bunch)

3 tablespoons plain
  whole milk Greek
  yogurt

LAYERING

2 tablespoons unsalted
  butter

2 large yellow onions,
  thinly sliced

Kosher salt

1 cup unsalted cashews

½ cup raisins

SERVING

Sliced cucumbers and
  tomatoes

Lime wedges

Chopped fresh cilantro

on a rimmed baking sheet to cool and dry it out. (Leave the cinnamon and cardamom pods in the rice.) Don't skip this baking sheet step—it helps you get fluffy, perfectly cooked rice in the biryani.

4. Make the onions for layering: Melt the butter over high heat in the skillet that's on the stove. Add the sliced onions, season generously with salt, and cook, stirring constantly, until the onions are deep golden, significantly shrunken, and caramelized, 15 to 20 minutes. (You may need to lower the heat to medium-high if the onions start to brown too quickly.) Scrape out the onions into a small bowl and set aside. Wipe the skillet with a paper towel.

5. Brown the lamb: Add the oil to the same skillet over medium-high heat. Add half of the lamb chunks to the skillet, season them generously with salt, and brown the chunks on 2 sides, 3 to 5 minutes per side. Using tongs or a slotted spoon, transfer the lamb to a 5- to 7-quart slow cooker. Repeat with the remaining lamb.

6. Finish the masala: Put the cilantro, mint, and yogurt into the blender with the onion mixture. Season with 1 teaspoon salt and blend until smooth. Taste the sauce and add more salt if necessary. It should taste on the well-salted end of the spectrum because this sauce is going to season your rice, too. Scrape the sauce into the slow cooker with the lamb and stir to combine.

7. Assemble the biryani: Scatter half the cashews and raisins on the lamb. Spoon all the rice into an even layer on top. Scatter the remaining cashews and raisins and all of the caramelized onion over the top. Cover the insert tightly with foil, sealing it all the way around, and close the lid. Cook on LOW for 4 hours.

8. Turn the slow cooker off and let it stand, covered, for 5 minutes. Bring the covered insert to the table (or bring the whole slow cooker if your insert doesn't remove from the casing) and then carefully uncover the biryani and enjoy the fragrant steam. Serve the biryani from the insert, with sliced cucumbers and tomatoes on the side, and pass around the lime wedges and cilantro for topping.

Does not hold well on warm	Prep time: 1 hour 15 minutes	Slow-cook time: 4 hours	Equipment: 5- to 7-quart slow cooker

Cilantro, Mint, and Green
Chile Lamb Biryani, 172

Harissa Pork Chili with Toppings Galore

Everyone already knows you can make ground beef chili in the slow cooker, and there are countless good recipes for that. I wanted to offer something a little bit different, but that still hits those classic notes: creamy beans; rich, tender meat; thick, spicy broth. That brings us here: cannellini beans, braised pork, and a punchy harissa broth. And of course everyone's favorite thing about chili is the toppings bar. Here, it's a Middle Eastern–inspired spread of turmeric-tinted yogurt, slivers of preserved lemon, and some other crunchy, salty, pickle-y, herbed options. You can make it as elaborate or simple as you want, so feel free to edit this list as you like. Even a few options, such as fresh herbs, crumbled cheese, and crunchy crumbled chips, will make it feel like a party.

1 pound dried cannellini beans

2 tablespoons olive oil

2½ pounds boneless pork shoulder, trimmed of excess fat and cut into 1-inch pieces

Kosher salt

1 large red or yellow onion, chopped

5 garlic cloves, chopped

½ cup harissa, plus more if necessary

3 tablespoons tomato paste

2 teaspoons ground cumin

2 teaspoons smoked paprika

½ teaspoon ground cinnamon

3 thyme sprigs

2 large carrots, sliced 1 inch thick

1. Cover the beans by at least 1 inch of water in a large saucepan. Bring to a boil, then lower the heat to medium-low and cook at a bare simmer for at least 10 minutes while you prep the rest of the chili.

2. Meanwhile, warm the oil in a large skillet over high heat. Add half the pork, spread it out evenly in the skillet, season it generously with salt, and let it cook undisturbed so it lightly browns, about 5 minutes. Stir to flip the pieces and repeat. With a slotted spoon, transfer the pork to a 6- to 8-quart slow cooker. Repeat with the remaining pork.

3. Reduce the heat under the skillet to medium-high. Add the onion, season generously with salt, and cook, stirring occasionally, until the onion is softened and starting to brown, about 8 minutes. Add the garlic and cook until fragrant and softened, 2 minutes. Stir in the harissa and tomato paste and cook, stirring, until combined, 1 minute. Add the cumin, paprika, and cinnamon and cook, stirring, until fragrant, about 30 seconds. Add 3 cups water, increase the heat to high, and wait for the water to come to a simmer, stirring and scraping up the browned bits on the bottom of the pan.

4. Pour the mixture into the slow cooker. Add 2 more cups water, the thyme, carrots, bay leaves, lemon zest and juice, and 1 tablespoon salt and stir to combine. Drain the beans and add them to the slow cooker; stir to combine. Cover and cook until the beans and pork are tender, about 9 hours on LOW or 6 hours on HIGH.

2 bay leaves

Finely grated zest and juice of 1 lemon, plus more lemon juice if necessary

¾ cup finely chopped fresh flat-leaf parsley

1 tablespoon thyme leaves

1 cup plain whole milk or 2% Greek yogurt

¾ teaspoon ground turmeric

Slivered preserved lemon rind; coarsely crushed pita chips; crumbled feta cheese; chopped fresh parsley, dill, and cilantro; sliced scallions; and/or beet-pickled turnips, for topping (see note, at right)

5. Remove the thyme sprigs and bay leaves and discard. Stir in the parsley and the thyme leaves. Cover and keep cooking on LOW or WARM for a few minutes.

6. Season the yogurt with a bit of salt and stir in the turmeric. Taste the stew and add more salt, harissa, or lemon juice as needed. Set the seasoned yogurt and other toppings out in little bowls and serve the stew from the cooker.

Good to know: You can find brilliant pink beet-pickled turnips and preserved lemons at any Middle Eastern market. To use the pickled turnips in the toppings bar, thinly slice or dice them. To use the lemons, rinse them and cut away the inner flesh, then very thinly slice the rind.

| ALL-DAY | Holds well on warm through step 4 for up to 2 hours | Prep time: 30 minutes | Slow-cook time: 6 hours or 9 hours |
| | | Finish time: 15 minutes | Equipment: 6- to 8-quart slow cooker |

Sticky Gochujang Pork Shoulder and All the Fixings

MAKES 8 TO 10 SERVINGS

This meat fest is loosely inspired by Korean bo ssam. *Serve the big platter of pork with side dishes of cooked white rice and a few varieties of kimchi, and a bunch of lettuce leaves for wrapping. It's basically a one-stop dinner party—just set everything out and let everyone help themselves, family style. To drink, offer small glasses of chilled* sochu—*a Korean rice spirit—if you can find it.*

One 5- to 6-pound skinless pork shoulder, bone in or out (bone-in will yield closer to 8 servings; bone-out will yield closer to 10)

Kosher salt

¾ cup *gochujang* (see note, page 130)

⅓ cup sugar

5 garlic cloves, minced or grated

One 3-inch ginger knob, peeled and grated (about 3 tablespoons)

2 tablespoons sesame seeds

1 teaspoon red pepper flakes

Assorted lettuce leaves, for wrapping

Kimchi, sliced cucumbers, and white rice (about 1 cooked cup per person), for serving

1. Pat the pork dry and put it into a 6- to 8-quart slow cooker. Season it lightly with salt on all sides. (*Gochujang* is salty, so you don't need as much salt as you usually would for a big hunk of meat.)

2. Combine the *gochujang*, sugar, garlic, ginger, sesame seeds, and red pepper flakes in a small bowl and mix well. Pour the *gochujang* mixture over the pork, rubbing the seasoning into the pork on all sides with your hands. Cook until the pork is tender, about 6 hours on HIGH (recommended for the extra caramelization) or 9 hours on LOW.

3. Using tongs, remove the pork from the braising liquid and put it on a cutting board to rest. Pour the braising liquid into a large liquid measuring cup—let it settle for a minute and then ladle up and discard the clear fat that rises to the top. (There will be a lot of it.) Pour the rest of the liquid into a medium saucepan and bring it to a simmer over medium-high heat. Let it bubble away until it's reduced by half and looks saucy, about 15 minutes.

4. Meanwhile, cut and pull the pork into thick slices and chunks. There's no need to be careful about it; you just want to end up with a bunch of big slices and pieces so that there's plenty of porky surface area to caramelize in the broiler. (Discard the bone if there is one.)

Recipe continues on page 182.

See the photo on pages 180–181.

5. Line a rimmed baking sheet with parchment. Put the pork on the prepared baking sheet and drizzle it all over with the reduced sauce, tossing to coat. Set the broiler on high and position a rack 6 inches from the heat source (if that's how your broiler works). Broil the pork until deeply browned in spots, about 5 minutes. Rotate the baking sheet if necessary to get all the pieces caramelized. Put the pork on a serving platter along with lettuce for wrapping. Put out bowls of kimchi, cucumbers, and rice.

Good to know: *You can braise the pork up to 2 days ahead and refrigerate it in a sealed container. Then lift the hardened fat off the top and discard it. Pick up the recipe in the middle of step 3: Reduce the braising liquid and then caramelize the pork under the broiler. If you have leftover pork, chop it up and stir-fry it with the leftover rice and chopped leftover kimchi, plus an egg, for the most delicious fried rice.*

ALL-DAY	Holds well on warm through step 2 for up to 2 hours	Prep time: 10 minutes	Slow-cook time: 6 hours or 9 hours
		Finish time: 30 minutes	Equipment: 6- to 8-quart slow cooker

Za'atar Roast Chicken with Tahini Panzanella

MAKES 4 SERVINGS

This centerpiece roast chicken is flavored with za'atar, a Middle Eastern spice blend that's herbal, rich, and tangy all at once thanks to thyme, sesame seeds, and sumac. "Roasting" a chicken in the slow cooker results in tender, juicy meat but flabby skin, which is easily fixed with a quick run under the broiler after the chicken is carved. Serve the chicken pieces on top of the herb-heavy, tahini-dressed panzanella, or bread salad.

CHICKEN

2 tablespoons *za'atar*

1 tablespoon ground sumac

Kosher salt

One 4- to 5-pound chicken, patted dry

PANZANELLA

One 12- to 14-ounce rustic crusty sesame loaf, cut roughly into 1- to 2-inch cubes

2 tablespoons olive oil

2 pints cherry tomatoes, quartered

4 scallions, white and light green parts, trimmed and sliced

1 bunch of fresh flat-leaf parsley, leaves chopped

1 bunch of fresh dill, leaves chopped

1. Set an empty 5- to 8-quart slow cooker on **HIGH**. Mix together the *za'atar*, sumac, and 2 teaspoons salt in a small bowl and rub the mixture all over the chicken, including under the skin of the breasts. (Just gently loosen the skin from the breast meat by running your fingers under the skin and get some of the spice mixture up in there.)

2. Put the chicken in the slow cooker breast up, cover, and reduce the heat to **LOW**. Cook until the internal temperature of the chicken reaches 160°F in the breast and 165°F in the fattest part of the thigh when checked with an instant-read or probe thermometer, 5 to 6 hours.

3. Make the *panzanella*: About 1 hour before serving, preheat the oven to 325°F. Spread the bread cubes on a rimmed baking sheet, toss with the oil, and bake until just crisp and dry but not browned, 20 minutes. Put the bread cubes into a large shallow serving bowl. Line the same baking sheet with parchment paper and set aside.

4. Add the tomatoes, scallions, parsley, dill, and tarragon to the bowl with the bread. In a small bowl, whisk together the lemon juice and tahini. If your tahini is thick, you might need a little warm water to thin the dressing; add it a spoonful at a time until the dressing is creamy and pourable. Season the dressing with salt and pepper, then pour it over the *panzanella* and toss well. Taste, season with salt and pepper, and toss again. Set aside.

1 bunch of fresh
   tarragon, leaves
   chopped

¼ cup fresh lemon juice

¼ cup tahini

Kosher salt and freshly
   ground black pepper

5. Using your hands and a pair of tongs slung through the chicken's cavity, transfer the chicken to a cutting board to rest. Set the broiler on high and position a rack 6 inches from the heat source (if that's how your broiler works).

6. Carve the chicken and set the pieces skin side up on the prepared baking sheet. Broil the chicken for 5 to 10 minutes, very much depending on the strength of your broiler, watching closely and rotating the pan if necessary to get all the skin crisp and golden. Serve the chicken on top of the *panzanella*.

Does not hold well on warm	Prep time: 5 minutes	Slow-cook time: 5 to 6 hours
	Finish time: 45 minutes	Equipment: 5- to 8-quart slow cooker

Sticky Toffee Pudding with Maple Caramel

Desserts

Slow cookers can make terrific desserts—in fact, in some cases, sweets made in the slow cooker are better or more foolproof than those made in the oven. There are a few techniques that work beautifully: You can use a slow cooker as a water bath or a steam oven, the former to make custards—like cheesecake and pots de crème—and the latter to make very moist steamed cakes, such as upside-down cake and sticky toffee pudding. You can also use it to braise or poach fruit for compotes. If you had asked me a couple of years ago, I would have said slow-cooker desserts are more likely to be gimmicky than good. I hope these recipes will change your mind, as they have mine.

*All-day recipes: These recipes can cook or hold on warm unattended for 8 hours or more.

Sticky Toffee Pudding with Maple Caramel

Sticky toffee pudding is a rich British dessert that's basically an exceptionally moist date cake with caramel sauce poured over the top. Steaming in the slow cooker is an absolutely foolproof way to make it, and this recipe is heavily adapted from one from Food Network Kitchen. The hazard of STP is that it can be too sweet, with the honeyed taste of the dates combined with even more sugar in the cake. I balance all that sweetness by first cooking the dates with strong coffee, an idea I got from Her Majesty Martha Stewart. You don't taste the coffee in the finished cake, but there is a dark, bitter-edged complexity left behind that's just perfect. The maple syrup in the easy caramel sauce is also an unorthodox American addition—but maple goes so well with dates.

PUDDING

8 ounces pitted Medjool dates (15 to 16 large dates), finely chopped

½ cup strong brewed coffee

½ teaspoon baking soda

1¼ cups all-purpose flour

1½ teaspoons baking powder

½ teaspoon kosher salt

½ teaspoon freshly ground nutmeg

½ teaspoon ground cardamom

¼ teaspoon ground cloves

⅓ cup pure maple syrup

⅓ cup packed light brown sugar

1. Make the pudding: Put the dates into a small saucepan and cover them with the coffee. Bring the mixture to a boil over medium heat and let it boil, stirring and mashing the dates with the back of a spoon, until the dates have absorbed most of the coffee and formed a paste, about 3 minutes. Remove the pot from the heat and stir in the baking soda. The mixture will foam a little. Set aside.

2. In a medium bowl, stir together the flour, baking powder, salt, nutmeg, cardamom, and cloves. In a large bowl, whisk the maple syrup, sugar, melted butter, and eggs until smooth. Stir the date-coffee mixture into the maple syrup mixture, then stir in the dry ingredients until just combined.

3. Pour 4 cups water into the bottom of a 6- to 8-quart slow cooker. Pour the batter into a 2-quart soufflé or baking dish that fits into your slow cooker, then set the baking dish into the cooker. (The water should come about halfway up the side of the dish.) Place a double layer of paper towels over the top of the cooker to soak up condensation, leaving some overhang so that the paper towels don't fall onto the pudding, and then close the lid on top of the paper towels (see page xx for a how-to). Cook on LOW until the pudding is just firm and set on top, 4 hours.

8 tablespoons (1 stick) unsalted butter, melted

2 large eggs

Whipped cream, for serving

SAUCE

1½ cups pure maple syrup

½ cup heavy cream

½ teaspoon salt

4. Make the sauce: Bring the maple syrup to a boil in a small saucepan. Immediately lower the heat to medium-low to prevent it from boiling over. Simmer gently for 5 minutes, swirling occasionally but not stirring. Pour in the cream and salt, stir, and simmer gently for another 5 minutes.

5. Remove the pudding from the slow cooker and poke holes all over it with a skewer or cake tester. A little at a time, pour half of the sauce over the top of the pudding and let it soak in. Serve the pudding warm with whipped cream and the rest of the sauce on the side.

Good to know: Like the banana cake on page 190, this pudding is best served warm. If you want to make it ahead, let it cool before covering it with plastic wrap and storing at room temperature. Make the sauce just before serving.

Does not hold well on warm	Prep time: 15 minutes	Slow-cook time: 4 hours
	Finish time: 15 minutes	Equipment: 6- to 8-quart slow cooker and a 2-quart soufflé or baking dish (even a loaf pan) that fits inside the cooker

Coconut Banana Cake with Brown Butter Caramel Sauce

This makes a very moist cake, in the style of a steamed British pudding, with tropical flavors of banana and coconut. The sprinkle of pecans adds welcome crunch.

CAKE

1¼ cups all-purpose flour

1½ teaspoons baking powder

1 teaspoon ground cardamom

1 teaspoon ground cinnamon

½ teaspoon baking soda

½ teaspoon kosher salt

3 large eggs

½ cup granulated sugar

⅓ cup pure maple syrup

8 tablespoons (1 stick) unsalted butter, melted and slightly cooled

3 very ripe medium bananas, mashed

⅓ cup well-shaken full-fat coconut milk

1 teaspoon pure vanilla extract

1. Make the cake: In a medium bowl, stir together the flour, baking powder, cardamom, cinnamon, baking soda, and salt. In a large bowl, whisk the eggs, granulated sugar, and maple syrup until evenly combined and smooth, then whisk in the melted butter, mashed bananas, coconut milk, and vanilla. Add the dry ingredients to the wet and stir until just combined into a uniform batter.

2. Pour 4 cups water into a 6- to 8-quart slow cooker. Pour the batter into a 2-quart soufflé or baking dish that fits into your slow cooker, then set the dish into the cooker. (The water should come about halfway up the side of the dish.) Place a double layer of paper towels over the top of the cooker to soak up condensation, leaving some overhang so that the paper towels don't fall on the cake, and then close the lid on top of the paper towels (see page xx for a how-to). Cook on LOW until the cake is just firm and set on top, 4 hours.

3. Just before serving, make the sauce: Melt the butter in a medium skillet over medium-high heat and cook, swirling occasionally, until the butter foams and the butter solids turn dark golden brown, 3 to 5 minutes. The

6 tablespoons unsalted butter

⅓ cup well-shaken full-fat coconut milk

⅓ cup packed dark brown sugar

2 ripe medium bananas, sliced about ¼ inch thick

Pinch of kosher salt

Vanilla ice cream, for topping

½ cup pecans, toasted (page 72) and chopped, for topping

butter should smell nutty and caramelized. Immediately reduce the heat to medium and stir in the coconut milk and brown sugar. The mixture will bubble and sputter. Stir constantly until the sugar dissolves and a creamy caramel sauce forms, about 1 minute. Add the sliced bananas and salt and cook for just a few seconds, gently stirring to coat the bananas in the caramel without mashing them. Remove from the heat.

4. Serve the cake warm, topped with the warm sauce, ice cream, and toasted pecans.

Good to know: The cake is best warm, a few minutes after it comes out of the cooker, but it's also good at room temperature. You can make the cake up to a day in advance of serving; let it cool completely, then cover the top with plastic wrap and store at room temperature. Make the sauce just before serving.

Does not hold well on warm	Prep time: 20 minutes	Slow-cook time: 4 hours
	Finish time: 15 minutes	Equipment: 6- to 8-quart slow cooker and a 2-quart soufflé or baking dish (even a loaf pan) that fits inside the cooker

Coconut-Rose Jasmine Rice Pudding

I love coconut and rosewater together; it's a common combination in Indian and Middle Eastern sweets. I know it seems odd to call for light coconut milk in a dessert, but full-fat coconut milk makes the pudding gummy after chilling. The coconut flavor is boosted with coconut water as well as dried coconut chips. If you have access to freshly grated coconut, that would be even better. Some people are more sensitive to rosewater's perfume-y quality than others, so if you're not completely sold, add just ¼ teaspoon.

1 cup jasmine rice, well rinsed

Two 14-ounce cans light coconut milk

2⅓ cups coconut water

1 cup unsweetened dried coconut chips or flakes

1 cup raw turbinado or demerara sugar or ½ cup granulated sugar

1 tablespoon pure vanilla extract

½ teaspoon kosher salt

2 tablespoons unsalted butter

½ teaspoon rosewater

Dried rose petals, chopped pistachios, and/or diced mango, for topping

Generously grease a 5- to 8-quart slow cooker. Combine the rice, coconut milk, coconut water, coconut chips, sugar, vanilla, and salt in the cooker and stir to combine. Cover and cook on **HIGH** until the rice is creamy, 3 to 4 hours. Stir in the butter until melted, then the rosewater. Spoon into bowls and serve at room temperature or chilled with the desired toppings.

Good to know: A dried rose-petal topping makes rice pudding as beautiful as it's ever going to get; you can find food-grade rose petals on Amazon. But of course they aren't mandatory—the rose flavor comes from the rosewater.

Holds well on warm for a maximum of 1 hour	Prep time: 5 minutes	Slow-cook time: 3 to 4 hours
	Finish time: 5 minutes	Equipment: 5- to 8-quart slow cooker

Peach Rye Shortcakes with Ginger Sugar

The rye and ginger give these shortcakes an unexpected twist, but really, this recipe is supersimple: a slow-cooker peach compote served on easy drop biscuits with whipped cream. The rye shortbreads are adapted from a recipe by Yossy Arefi, who wrote the wonderful Sweeter Off the Vine *cookbook. The rye flour doesn't make the shortbreads taste like rye bread—not even a little bit. Instead, it gives a really lovely, almost floral, grainy flavor that's subtle and very delicious. I use raw turbinado or demerara sugar for the compote because it adds a more flavorful sweetness than granulated sugar. You can substitute light brown sugar if you prefer.*

PEACHES

4 pounds fresh ripe peaches (about 11 medium) or frozen peach slices, thawed and drained (if using frozen, thawed peaches, skip step 1)

1 cup raw turbinado or demerara sugar

1 tablespoon plus 1 teaspoon minute, quick, or instant tapioca

Juice of 1 lemon

½ teaspoon salt

1. If using fresh peaches, bring a large pot of water to a rolling boil. Fill a large bowl with ice water and set aside. On the bottom of each peach, using a paring knife, cut through the skin to make an X. Working 3 or 4 peaches at a time, drop the peaches into the boiling water for 30 seconds to 1 minute. Remove the peaches with a slotted spoon and drop them into the ice water. Repeat with the remaining peaches. Starting from the flaps of skin where you scored the bottom of the peaches, pull the skins from the peaches. They should peel easily. Halve the peaches, discard the pits, and slice the peach halves into about 8 slices each.

2. Add the peaches, sugar, tapioca, lemon juice, and salt to a 5- to 8-quart slow cooker and gently stir to combine. Cover and cook on LOW for 3 hours. Stir well, set the lid ajar by about 5 inches, and increase the heat to HIGH. Cook for 1 more hour, stirring occasionally if possible.

3. Meanwhile, make the biscuits: Preheat the oven to 450°F. In a small bowl, mix the turbinado sugar with 1 teaspoon of the ground ginger and the pinch of salt. Set aside.

2 tablespoons raw
   turbinado or
   demerara sugar

3 teaspoons ground
   ginger

1 pinch plus ¾ teaspoon
   kosher salt

1 cup all-purpose flour

1 cup rye flour

¼ cup granulated sugar

1 tablespoon baking
   powder

¼ teaspoon baking soda

8 tablespoons (1 stick)
   cold unsalted butter,
   cut into small bits

½ cup whole buttermilk

¼ cup heavy cream

1 egg yolk, beaten with
   1 teaspoon water

Whipped cream
   (optional)

4. In a large mixing bowl, stir together the all-purpose flour, rye flour, granulated sugar, baking powder, baking soda, the remaining 2 teaspoons ground ginger, and ¾ teaspoon salt. Add the butter and work it into the dry ingredients with your fingers, until the bits of butter are about the size of peas and are totally coated in flour. Add the buttermilk and cream and gently mix with your hands just until a sticky, uniform dough forms. (Try not to overmix.)

5. Drop the dough onto a baking sheet in small, round handfuls, making 8 biscuits total. Brush them with the beaten egg yolk–water mixture and sprinkle generously with the ginger–turbinado sugar mixture. (Use about two-thirds of the mixture to top the biscuits and keep the remaining ginger sugar for serving.) Bake until the biscuits are golden brown, 13 to 14 minutes. Let cool to room temperature on a rack.

6. To serve, cut the biscuits in half and put the biscuit bottoms on plates. Top with the peach compote, whipped cream, and a sprinkle of the remaining ginger sugar. Set the biscuit tops on and serve.

Good to know: You can make the compote up to 2 days in advance and serve it either warm or cold, though I think it's best warm. To reheat it, just put it into a medium saucepan over medium heat and stir it occasionally until it's warmed through.

Holds on warm through step 2 for a maximum of 1 hour	Prep time: 25 minutes	Slow-cook time: 4 hours
	Finish time: 15 minutes to make the biscuits, 15 minutes to bake them, plus cooling	Equipment: 5- to 8-quart slow cooker

Matcha-White Chocolate Pots de Crème

Matcha is a green tea powder that has a vibrant green color and a grassy, sweet flavor—it is wonderful paired with sweet, milky white chocolate in these silky custards.

3 large egg yolks

4 ounces white chocolate, finely chopped (about ¾ cup)

2 teaspoons sugar

½ teaspoon salt

1 tablespoon matcha powder

1 cup heavy cream

1 cup whole milk

1 teaspoon pure vanilla extract

Additional white chocolate, shaved with a vegetable peeler, for topping

1. Whisk together the egg yolks in a large (at least 4-cup) liquid measuring cup or spouted bowl and set aside. Put the white chocolate into a separate medium bowl. Pour 2 cups water into a 6-quart or larger slow cooker.

2. Combine the sugar and salt in a medium saucepan. Put the matcha into a fine-mesh strainer set over the saucepan and shake the strainer to sift the matcha into the saucepan. Set the strainer aside by resting it over the measuring cup holding the egg yolks. Stir together the sugar, salt, and matcha. Add the cream to the saucepan, a tiny bit at a time, whisking to incorporate each time. When you've added ½ cup or so of cream, you should have a uniform paste with no lumps. (If you simply added all the liquid at once, the matcha would clump up.) When you have a smooth paste, add the remaining cream and the milk, whisking to combine. Stir in the vanilla.

3. Turn the heat on medium-high and cook, whisking often, until the mixture just starts to simmer. (Watch it when it starts steaming, because once it boils, it will bubble over the sides of the pot quickly.) Pour the hot matcha mixture over the white chocolate in the bowl and let it sit for 3 minutes, then whisk until the chocolate is melted and the mixture is smooth. Pour the matcha–white chocolate mixture through the fine-mesh strainer set over the yolks, then immediately whisk well to combine. Divide the mixture evenly among six 4-ounce oven-safe ramekins.

4. Carefully place the ramekins into your slow cooker, making sure not to jostle any water into the ramekins. You might be able to set them all in the cooker in a single layer. If not, place 4 or 5 ramekins into the insert and then balance the remaining 1 or 2 ramekins on top of the others (see photo at right for setup). The water should come about halfway up the sides of the bottom layer of ramekins. Place a double layer of paper towels over the top of the insert to soak up condensation, leaving some overhang so that the paper towels don't fall onto the ramekins, and then close the lid on top of the paper towels (see page xx for a how-to). Cook on LOW for 2 hours 30 minutes, until the custards are set but still jiggly.

5. Turn off and uncover the slow cooker. Let the ramekins cool for a few minutes before removing them from the cooker. Let cool to room temperature before serving, topped with a bit of shaved white chocolate. Or, to chill them, let them cool completely, then cover with plastic wrap, pressing the plastic onto the surface of the custard to prevent it from forming a skin, and refrigerate for up to 2 days. Let them sit at room temperature for 10 minutes before topping with white chocolate and serving.

Good to know: You can buy matcha on Amazon or any shop that has a good tea selection.

Does not hold well on warm	Prep time: 20 minutes	Slow-cook time: 2 hours 30 minutes
	Finish time: Cooling/chilling	Equipment: 6-quart or larger slow cooker and six 4-ounce (½-cup) ramekins

This photo shows the pots before cooking. See the finished dessert on page 200.

Vietnamese Coffee Pots
de Crème and Matcha–White
Chocolate Pots de Crème, 197

Vietnamese Coffee Pots de Crème

Inspired by Vietnamese coffee, these dense custards are flavored with strong coffee and sweetened condensed milk. I use instant espresso powder because it has an intense taste and dissolves easily in milk—a huge flavor payoff for very little effort.

3 large egg yolks

One 14-ounce can sweetened condensed milk

1 cup whole milk

3 tablespoons instant espresso powder, such as Café Bustelo

¼ teaspoon kosher salt

Whipped cream, for serving

1. Whisk together the egg yolks in a large (at least 4-cup) measuring cup or spouted bowl and set aside. Pour 2 cups water into a 6-quart or larger slow cooker.

2. In a medium saucepan, combine the condensed milk, milk, espresso, and salt over medium-high heat and bring just to a boil, stirring often. Turn off the heat and let the milk mixture cool for 1 minute, then pour a little bit of the warm milk into the egg yolks, whisking constantly. Add the rest of the milk in a slow stream, whisking constantly. Divide the mixture evenly among six 4-ounce, oven-safe ramekins.

3. Carefully place the ramekins into your slow cooker, making sure not to jostle any water into the ramekins. You might be able to set them all into the cooker in a single layer. If not, place 4 or 5 ramekins into the insert and then balance the remaining 1 or 2 ramekins on top of the others (see photo on page 199). The water should come about halfway up the sides of the bottom layer of ramekins. Place a double layer of paper towels on top of the insert to soak up condensation, leaving some overhang so that the paper towels don't fall onto the ramekins, and then close the lid on top of the paper towels (see page xx for a how-to). Cook on LOW for 2 hours 30 minutes, until the custards are set but still jiggly.

4. Turn off and uncover the slow cooker. Let the ramekins cool for a few minutes before removing them from the cooker. Let them cool to room temperature before serving, topped with whipped cream. Or, to chill them, let them cool completely, then cover them with plastic wrap, pressing the plastic onto the surface of the custard to prevent it from forming a skin, and refrigerate for up to 2 days. Let them sit at room temperature for 10 minutes before topping with whipped cream and serving.

Does not hold well on warm	Prep time: 10 minutes	Slow-cook time: 2 hours 30 minutes
	Finish time: Cooling/chilling	Equipment: 6-quart or larger slow cooker and six 4-ounce (½-cup) ramekins

Honey-Poached Pears with Orange and Star Anise

4 almost-ripe or ripe Bartlett pears (2 to 2½ pounds), peeled, halved, cored, and stemmed

½ cup honey

2 whole star anise

1 teaspoon finely grated orange zest

Pinch of kosher salt

Vanilla ice cream, for serving (optional)

1. Combine all the ingredients in a 4- to 8-quart slow cooker and stir well to combine and coat the pears in the honey. Cover and cook on LOW for 1 hour to 1 hour 30 minutes—the riper the pears, the less time they should be cooked.

2. Remove the pears and the star anise from the cooking liquid with a slotted spoon and set them on a serving dish or into another container. Pour the cooking liquid into a small saucepan and bring it to a boil over high heat. Cook, stirring often, until slightly reduced, about 5 minutes. Pour the syrup over the pears and chill. Serve alone or with ice cream.

| Holds well on warm for up to 30 minutes | Prep time: 15 minutes | Slow-cook time: 1 hour 30 minutes |
| | Finish time: 5 minutes | Equipment: 4- to 8-quart slow cooker |

Cannoli Cheesecake with Biscotti Crust

When I was growing up, every time we went into Boston we stopped at Mike's Pastry in the North End for cannoli. In my memory, those cannoli—crisp, shattering shells and slightly grainy ricotta filling—were the be-all and end-all of desserts. So fancy! I especially loved the mini–chocolate chips decorating the exposed cream on either end. That almondy and lemony cannoli filling inspired this cheesecake.

4 ounces pistachio or almond biscotti

2 tablespoons unsalted butter, melted

12 ounces (1½ 8-ounce blocks) full-fat cream cheese (not cream cheese spread), at room temperature

12 ounces (1½ cups) whole milk ricotta, drained in a fine-mesh strainer, at room temperature

¾ cup sugar

1 teaspoon pure almond extract

1 teaspoon pure vanilla extract

Finely grated zest of ½ large lemon (about 2 teaspoons)

½ teaspoon kosher salt

3 large eggs, lightly beaten

Shelled unsalted pistachios and mini–chocolate chips, for topping

1. Pour 4 cups water into a 6- to 8-quart oval slow cooker or a 4- to 8-quart round slow cooker. Choose an oven-safe baking dish that fits in your slow cooker and holds at least 6 cups, such as a 2-quart soufflé dish or an 8½ × 4½-inch loaf pan. (If you have a round slow cooker, you must use a round baking dish, not a loaf pan.) To make sure you have the right amount of water in the cooker, try putting the empty baking dish in the slow cooker. The water should come about halfway up the sides of the dish, and the water should not threaten to slop into the dish. Add or remove water to get it to the right level.

2. Put the biscotti into a food processor and process until the cookies are in fine crumbs. Drizzle in the melted butter and pulse until the mixture looks like slightly wet sand. Press the biscotti mixture into the bottom of the baking dish or loaf pan, then put it in the fridge.

3. Rinse out the food processor and put the cream cheese, ricotta, sugar, almond and vanilla extracts, lemon zest, and salt into it. Process until combined and very smooth, about 1 minute, scraping down the sides at least once. Add the eggs and process just to fully combine, about 20 seconds, scraping down the sides once. (You don't want to beat the eggs too much because then they will cause the cheesecake to act a little like a soufflé—rising and then falling in the middle.)

4. Pour the filling into the prepared pan with the crust and set the pan in the slow cooker. Place a double layer of paper towels over the top of the cooker to soak up condensation, leaving some overhang so that the paper towels don't fall onto the cheesecake, and then close the lid on top of the

paper towels (see page xx for a how-to). Cook on **HIGH** until the cake is set but still a little jiggly in the middle, about 2 hours 30 minutes. Turn off and uncover the cooker and let the cheesecake cool a little so that you can lift it out. Let it cool completely at room temperature, then cover it with plastic and refrigerate for at least 1 hour and up to 2 days.

5. To remove the cheesecake from the baking dish or loaf pan, run a thin knife or spatula around the edges, then put a plate on top and flip the pan to invert the cheesecake onto the plate. Invert again onto another plate so the cake is right side up. Scatter pistachios and chocolate chips over the top and serve.

Good to know: For an even nicer look, like the one in the photo, melt the chocolate chips in a microwave or in a bowl set over a pan of simmering water. Put the chocolate into a small zip-top bag, seal the bag, snip a very small opening in one corner, and drizzle the melted chocolate in ribbons over the cake, then sprinkle on the pistachios.

Holds on warm for up to 30 minutes	Prep time: 25 minutes	Slow-cook time: 2 hours 30 minutes
Finish time: Cooling and 1 hour chilling	Equipment: 6- to 8-quart oval slow cooker or 4- to 8-quart round slow cooker and an oven-safe 2-quart baking or soufflé dish or 8½ × 4½-inch loaf pan that fits inside the cooker	

Dark Chocolate Cheesecake with Earl Grey Cream

MAKES 7 SERVINGS

These are really fun—everyone gets their own mini cheesecake. Dark chocolate (in the custard) and Earl Grey tea (in the cream) pair nicely—it's teatime in dessert form.

CHEESECAKES

4 ounces plain tea biscuits (cookies) or digestives, such as McVitie's, plus extra crumbled biscuits for serving (optional)

2 tablespoons unsalted butter, melted

One 3.5-ounce bar dark chocolate, broken into small bits

¾ cup heavy cream

2 pounds (four 8-ounce blocks) full-fat cream cheese (not cream cheese spread), at room temperature

1¼ cups sugar

2 tablespoons unsweetened cocoa powder

2 teaspoons pure vanilla extract

½ teaspoon kosher salt

3 large eggs, lightly beaten

1. Pour 5 cups water into a 6-quart or larger slow cooker. Put the biscuits into a food processor and process until you have fine crumbs. Pour in the melted butter and process until the mixture looks like slightly wet sand. Put about 1 heaping tablespoon of the crust mixture into seven 8-ounce jars, then lightly tamp it down to make a crust on the bottom of each jar. (The plastic pusher in the feed tube of the food processor is very useful for this.) Rinse out the food processor.

2. Put the dark chocolate into a medium bowl. Pour the cream into a small saucepan over medium-high heat. Bring the cream to a simmer, then pour it over the chocolate in the bowl and let it stand undisturbed for 3 minutes. Whisk until smooth.

3. Scrape the chocolate mixture into the food processor and add the cream cheese, sugar, cocoa powder, vanilla, and salt. Process until very smooth and evenly combined, about 1 minute, stopping to scrape down the sides at least once. Add the beaten eggs and process until just fully combined, scraping down the sides once, about 20 seconds. (You don't want to beat the eggs too much because then they will cause the cheesecake to act a little like a soufflé—rising and then falling in the middle.)

4. Divide the cheesecake mixture among the jars, leaving at least ½ inch headspace at the top. You can do this with a spoon or a ladle, or you can pour the mixture into a spouted measuring cup and pour from there, to make it easier. Carefully place the filled jars into the slow cooker, making sure not to jostle any water into the jars. They will fit snugly next to each other, but all 7 jars should fit in a 6-quart slow cooker. Place a double layer of paper towels over the top of the cooker to catch condensa-

1 cup heavy cream

3 Earl Grey tea bags

2 tablespoons
confectioners' sugar

tion, leaving some overhang so that the paper towels don't fall onto the cheesecakes, and then close the lid on top of the paper towels (see page xx for a how-to). Cook on **HIGH** until the cakes are set but still a little jiggly in the middle, about 1 hour 45 minutes to 2 hours.

5. Meanwhile, make the whipped cream: Bring the heavy cream to a simmer in a saucepan over medium-high heat. Add the tea bags and cook, stirring, about 30 seconds. Turn off the heat and let steep for 10 minutes. Squeeze the tea bags to release their liquid into the pot, then discard the tea bags. Cover and refrigerate until well chilled, at least 2 hours.

6. Turn off and uncover the cooker and let the cheesecakes cool a little so that you can lift them out. Let them cool completely at room temperature, then cover them with the lids or plastic wrap and refrigerate. The cakes are best refrigerated for at least 1 hour before eating, but they are ready to eat once cooled to room temperature. (They keep well refrigerated for about 2 days.)

7. When you're ready to serve the dessert, finish the Earl Grey whipped cream, whipping the cream to soft peaks with an electric mixer, then whipping in the confectioners' sugar just to combine. Serve the cheesecakes topped with the whipped cream and, if desired, a sprinkle of crumbled biscuits.

Does not hold well on warm	Prep time: 25 minutes	Slow-cook time: 1 hour 45 minutes to 2 hours
	Finish time: Cooling and chilling	Equipment: 6-quart or larger slow cooker and seven 8-ounce glass jars

Salted Dulce de Leche

You can make dulce de leche—*milky caramel—by boiling sealed cans of sweetened condensed milk. The milk reduces inside the can into a sticky, deliciously toasty caramel. It's easy to do on the stovetop, but you do need to monitor the water level—if it boils away, the cans can explode. That's not a concern in the slow cooker, because the water will not reduce in a significant way, making it completely hands-off. Ten hours of cooking results in a very dark, toasty, thick caramel that you can serve as a dessert dip. Adding flaky sea salt really makes the flavors pop. If there are leftovers, put a spoonful into your coffee in the morning.*

Two 14-ounce cans sweetened condensed milk

2 teaspoons to 1 tablespoon flaky sea salt, depending on how salty you like your caramel

Sliced apples, halved strawberries, pretzel rods, and/or tea biscuits, for dipping

1. Tear the labels off the cans. Put the cans on their sides in a 5- to 8-quart slow cooker. Cover the cans with water by 3 inches. Cover the cooker and cook on LOW for 10 hours.

2. Remove the cans with tongs and let them come to room temperature. (Don't try to open them while hot.) Once cool, open the cans and spoon the *dulce de leche* into a serving bowl. Stir in the salt and any other stir-ins (see Five Stir-In Ideas, below) that you'd like. Serve with the fruit, pretzels, and biscuits for dipping.

Good to know: You can make the dulce de leche *up to 3 days before serving, but you need to let it come fully to room temperature before serving or it will be too stiff.*

ALL-DAY	Holds well on warm through step 1 for up to 1 hours	Prep time: 5 minutes	Slow-cook time: 10 hours
		Finish time: 10 minutes	Equipment: 5- to 8-quart slow cooker

Five Stir-In Ideas

This caramel is luscious, deep, and very rich and sweet just the way it is. But if you want to gild the lily, here are a few ideas for stir-ins—you could use just one or a combination. You will want the *dulce de leche* to be at room temperature when you add these flavorings; when it's cold, it's too stiff to stir.

1 tablespoon dark rum

1 teaspoon finely grated citrus zest

Finely chopped salted peanuts

Finely chopped dark chocolate

The seeds scraped from 1 vanilla bean

Cardamom-Molasses Apple Upside-Down Cake

This exceptionally moist spice cake straddles the dessert-breakfast line. For dessert, serve it with ice cream or sweetened whipped cream. To take it more toward breakfast, substitute a whole grain flour for half (1 cup) of the all-purpose flour. You can use regular whole wheat flour, or try buckwheat flour, which is particularly good with the flavors in this cake.

APPLES

2 sweet-tart medium to large apples (about 1 pound), such as Honeycrisp, peeled, cored, and thinly sliced

½ cup packed light brown sugar

3 tablespoons unsalted butter

1 teaspoon ground cardamom

CAKE

2 cups all-purpose flour

1 teaspoon baking soda

1 teaspoon ground cardamom

1 teaspoon ground cinnamon

½ teaspoon baking powder

½ teaspoon kosher salt

¾ cup packed light brown sugar

1. Prepare the slow cooker: Fold a large piece of foil into a 3 × 12-inch strip and line 1 side of a 5- to 6-quart slow cooker's insert with the strip. Repeat to make a second strip and line the other side (see page xxv for a how-to). This foil collar will protect the sides of the cake from burning. Then line the entire insert with 1 piece of parchment, making sure the parchment comes up at least 2 inches on all sides (see page xxvi for a how-to). This is to prevent sticking and also to make it easier to reach in and remove the cake.

2. Make the apple layer: Put the apple slices into the prepared insert, spreading them out evenly. Combine the sugar, butter, and cardamom in a small saucepan and cook, stirring, until the butter and sugar melt into a syrup, about 3 minutes. Pour the syrup over the apples and stir to evenly combine.

3. Make the cake: Combine the flour, baking soda, cardamom, cinnamon, baking powder, and salt in a medium bowl. In a large bowl, beat together the brown sugar and butter with an electric mixer on high speed until the mixture is fluffy and lightened in color, about 2 minutes, scraping down the bowl as necessary. Beat in the egg and vanilla, then the molasses and yogurt, and beat until creamy and evenly combined. Decrease the mixer speed to medium-low and add the dry ingredients to the wet in 2 batches, beating between batches. Beat until the batter is just combined. Pour the cake batter over the apples and evenly spread over the top. Place a double layer of paper towels over the top of the cooker to soak up any condensation, leaving some overhang so that the paper towels don't fall onto the cake batter, and then close the lid on top of the paper

8 tablespoons (1 stick)
unsalted butter, at
room temperature

1 large egg

2 teaspoons pure vanilla
extract

½ cup unsulphured
molasses

½ cup plain whole milk
Greek yogurt

towels (see page xx for a how-to). Cook on HIGH for 2 hours, until the cake is set on top.

4. Uncover the slow cooker and turn it off. Let the cake rest for about 10 minutes. Grabbing the edges of the parchment liner, lift the cake out of the insert and set it on a cutting board. Put a serving plate or another cutting board over the top and flip to invert the cake so that the apples are on top. Carefully remove the parchment (so as not to dislodge the apples) and serve. Store the cake in an airtight container at room temperature for up to 2 days.

Good to know: I like this cake baked directly in the slow cooker insert (as opposed to a separate baking dish, as I do in other recipes) because it gives the cake a large top surface area for the caramelized apples. There is only one potential drawback: A slow cooker is heated with electrical coils that wind around the insert, and this means that the outer edge of a cake (the part touching the walls of the insert) can cook too quickly and get too dark. That's why it's important to line the insert walls with a foil collar—it acts like insulation, mitigating the heat and keeping the sides from burning. So, even though it's a tiny bit fussy, that step actually only takes a couple minutes, and it'll ensure that the edges of this lovely cake don't scorch.

Does not hold well on warm	Prep time: 20 minutes	Slow-cook time: 2 hours
	Finish time: 10 minutes	Equipment: 5- to 6-quart slow cooker

Universal Conversion Chart

OVEN TEMPERATURE EQUIVALENTS

250°F = 120°C

275°F = 135°C

300°F = 150°C

325°F = 160°C

350°F = 180°C

375°F = 190°C

400°F = 200°C

425°F = 220°C

450°F = 230°C

475°F = 240°C

500°F = 260°C

MEASUREMENT EQUIVALENTS

Measurements should always be level unless directed otherwise.

⅛ TEASPOON = 0.5 ML

¼ TEASPOON = 1 ML

½ TEASPOON = 2 ML

1 TEASPOON = 5 ML

1 TABLESPOON = 3 TEASPOONS = ½ FLUID OUNCE = 15 ML

2 TABLESPOONS = ⅛ CUP = 1 FLUID OUNCE = 30 ML

4 TABLESPOONS = ¼ CUP = 2 FLUID OUNCES = 60 ML

5⅓ TABLESPOONS = ⅓ CUP = 3 FLUID OUNCES = 80 ML

8 TABLESPOONS = ½ CUP = 4 FLUID OUNCES = 120 ML

10⅔ TABLESPOONS = ⅔ CUP = 5 FLUID OUNCES = 160 ML

12 TABLESPOONS = ¾ CUP = 6 FLUID OUNCES = 180 ML

16 TABLESPOONS = 1 CUP = 8 FLUID OUNCES = 240 ML

Dark Chocolate
Cheesecake with
Earl Grey Cream, 207,
after cooking

Acknowledgments

Thanks to Jonah Straus, who is always up for a conversation about ideas and who believed in this book and made it happen. And to Cassie Jones, a kindred cooking spirit and whip-smart editor with an infectious enthusiasm for slow-cooked cheesecake. Thank you to Andrew and Carrie Purcell, the most talented (and nicest) team in the business, and to Paige Hicks: You made this book look more beautiful than I could have imagined. (I want to write another cookbook just so I can do another shoot with you.)

Thank you to the talented and dedicated publicity, marketing, and design teams at William Morrow, and to Kara Zauberman, who is a pleasure. And to the extended *Food & Wine* family, past and present, particularly Tina Ujlaki, Dana Cowin, Pam Kaufman, and Yaran Noti. And specially Kristin Donnelly, who is so generous with her knowledge. Big thanks to Grant Achatz, Amy Thielen, Marcus Samuelsson, and Molly Yeh for your support of this book.

Thank you to meticulous, smart, talented recipe testers Mandy Maxwell, Kathryn Anible, and Julia Heffelfinger. And thank you to all the wonderful people who took in my leftovers, tried my recipes, and gave me their honest opinions. You've made the book so much better: Kathleen, Patrick, Trinidad, and Kingston Bennett; Stacey, Gabi, Lucia, and Avi Gillett; Miriam, Martin, and Oren Coleman; Gretchen VanEsselstyn; Andrea Lynn; Nicole Rende; Kaela Wohl; Krista Bernardone; and Cindy Felix. Thanks to my parents-in-law, Anil and Jyotsna Mhatre, for your support and for teaching Amol how to cook so well! And thanks to Jenny Hellman and Colette Eastwood, who are always interested in talking recipes.

Thanks to Lucy Charles and all the wonderful women at Les Bijoux de Miley for providing expert, loving childcare so that my husband and I can work.

To my parents, Phyllis Eastwood and Mario DiGregorio, both of whom are gone now: You taught me the value of hard work, the joy of a life filled with books, and that love is the only thing that matters. Thank you. And to Amol and Mira, my big loves, you make the whole world brighter and sweeter.

Index

Page numbers in italics indicate photos